The Land Conservancy of McHenry County

2016

Art of the Land Amateur Photography Contest Catalog

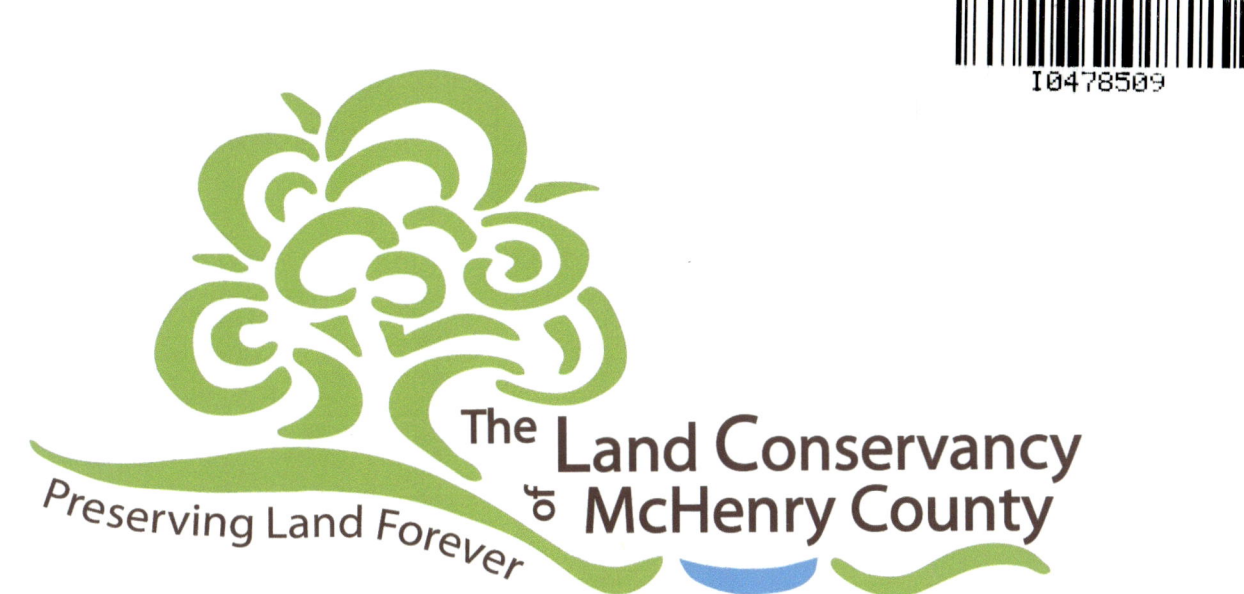

The Land Conservancy of McHenry County

Preserving Land Forever

The Mission:

To preserve natural, agricultural, and scenic land forever in and around McHenry County by working with landowners, communities and others of like-mind.

About The Land Conservancy of McHenry County

The Land Conservancy of McHenry County (TLC) has worked with over 100 landowners to preserve over 2,100 acres of land across McHenry County. Protected properties range from less than 1 acre to 250 acres in size. Preserved lands include high quality wetland and woodland habitat, farmland, scenic vistas, historic farmsteads, and similar valuable land resources.

The organization accomplishes most of its land preservation work by working with individuals who donate permanent conservation restrictions (also called conservation easements) on their land. Occasionally, individuals donate land to TLC and, from time to time, TLC purchases land, but only when that is the only conservation option available.

TLC is a local 501(c)(3) nonprofit organization recognized by the IRS and the State of Illinois since 1991. The organization is funded by members, grants, and fundraising events like Art of the Land.

TLC's Vision

The Land Conservancy of McHenry County's vision for the future of McHenry County is that this will be a community whose people take care of their home - McHenry County - by conserving land and water resources for all generations to come.

Share the Vision!

TLC is a nonprofit, member-supported organization. Joining is easy. Just visit the website **www.ConserveMC.org** and click on "Get Involved," or come by the office to make a membership donation. The office is located at Hennen Conservation Area, 4622 Dean Street, Woodstock. Please stop in and say hello!

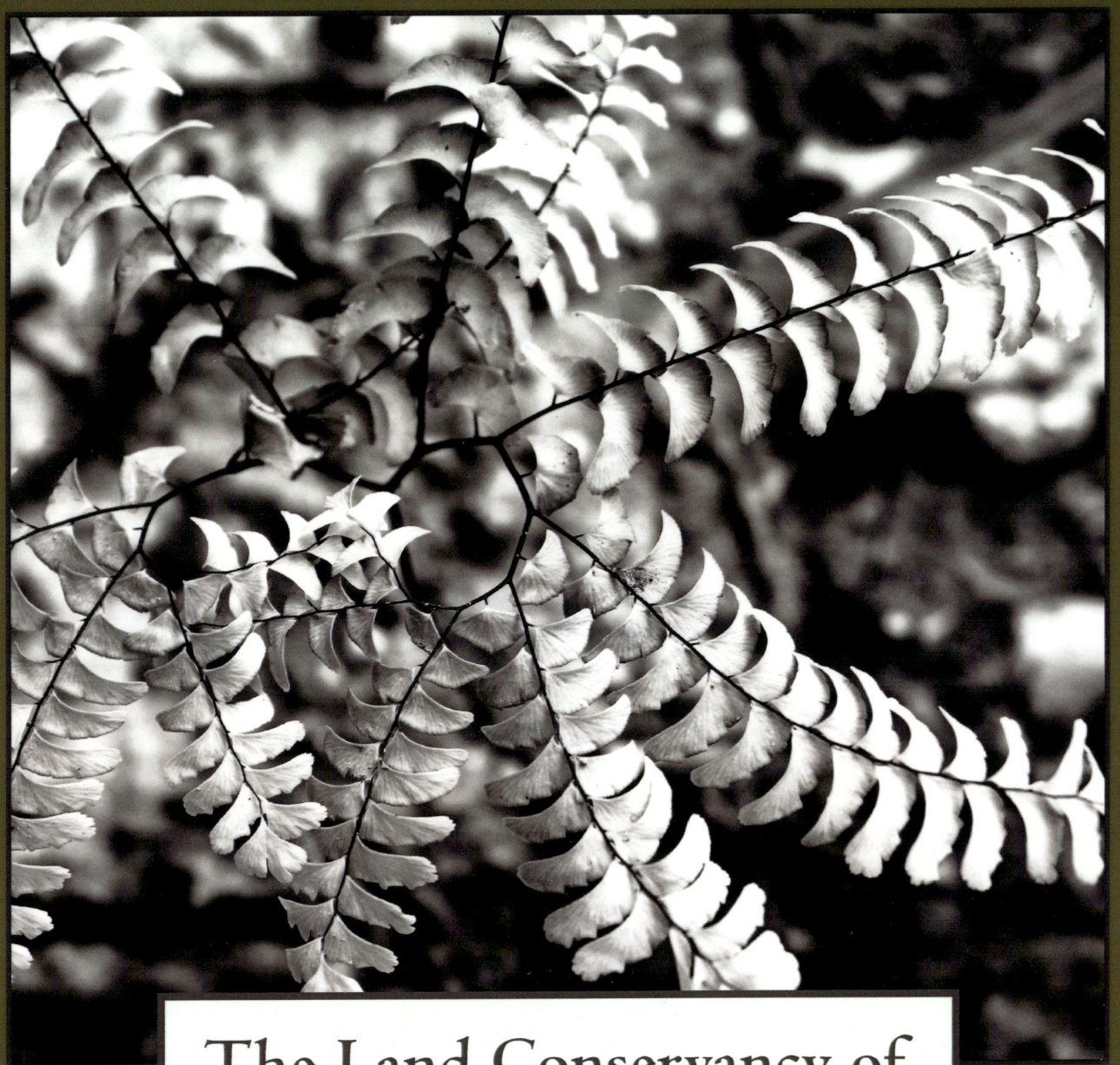

The Land Conservancy of McHenry County 2016 Photo Contest Catalog

ART OF THE LAND

Acorn Lane Conservation Area, Lake in the Hills

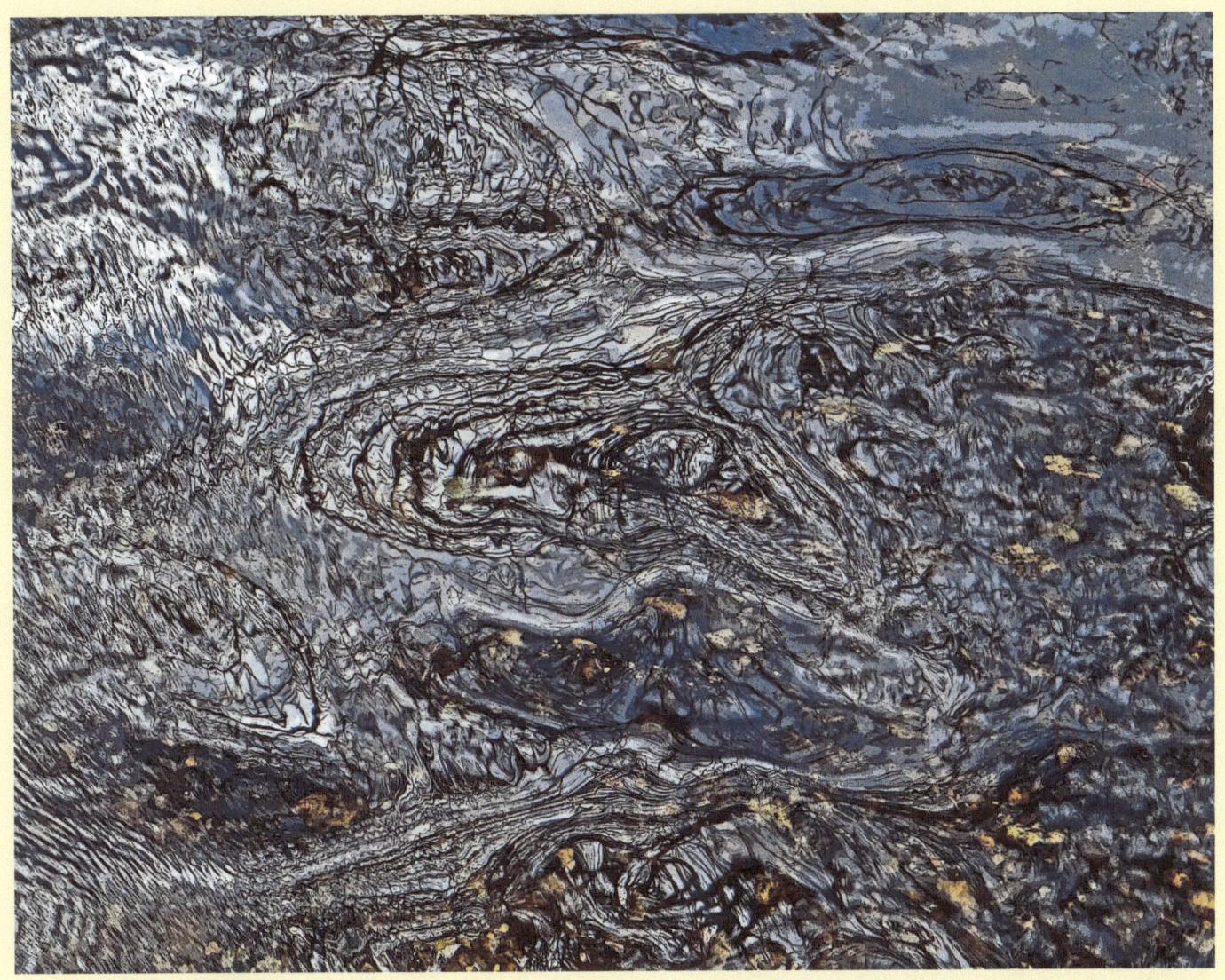

Photographer: Paul McFadden
13 acres donated to TLC in 2006

If you drive down Randall Road, you will see our sign declaring "This Land is Preserved Forever!" The complex of wetlands, prairies, and recent oak plantings will always be here providing habitat and beauty.

Acorn Lane Conservation Area, Lake in the Hills
Honorable Mention

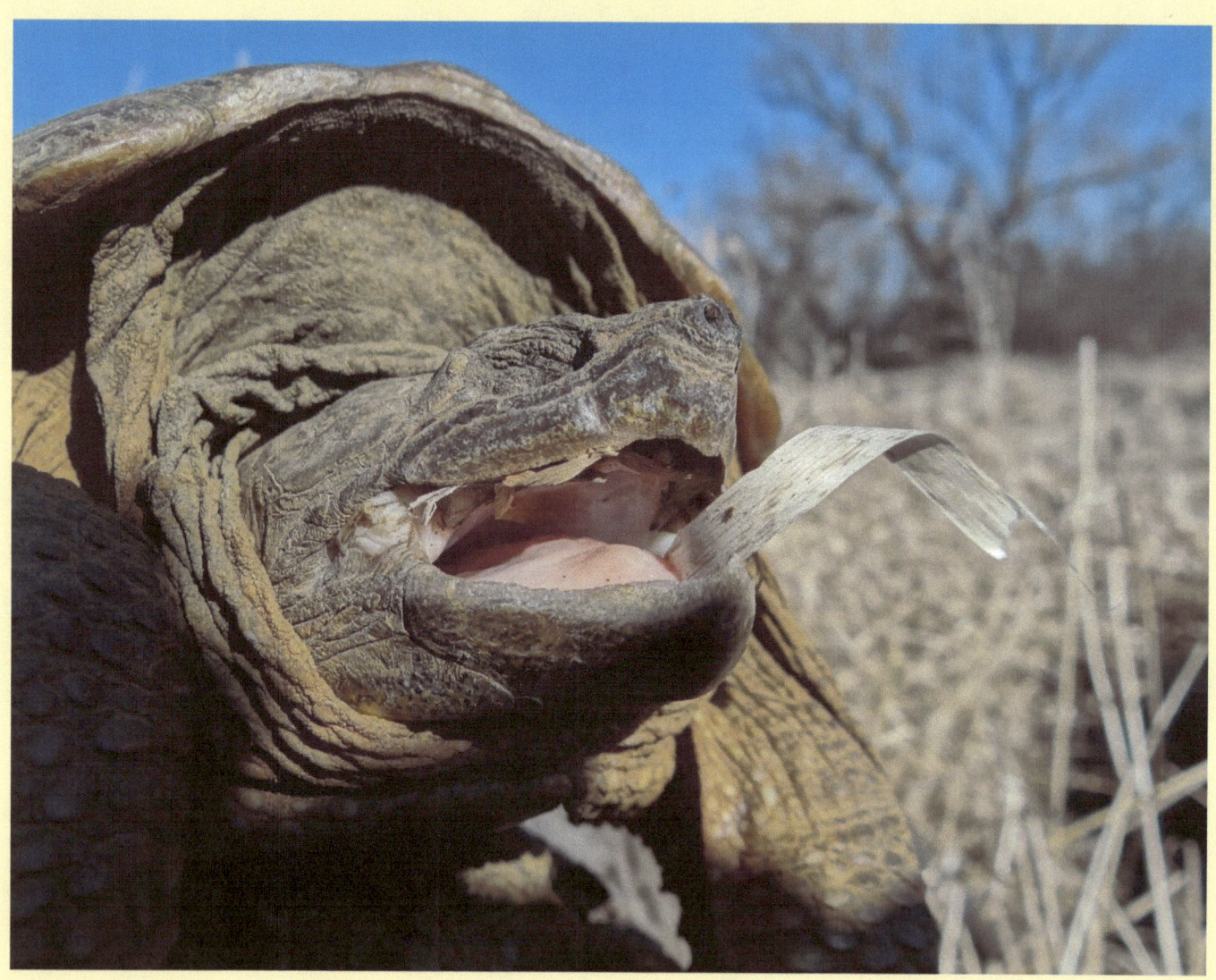

Photographer: Paul McFadden
13 acres donated to TLC in 2006

This preserve protects a section of Woods Creek and the surrounding wetland, allowing it to stay natural in a heavily developed area.

Anderson Conservation Easement, Nunda Township

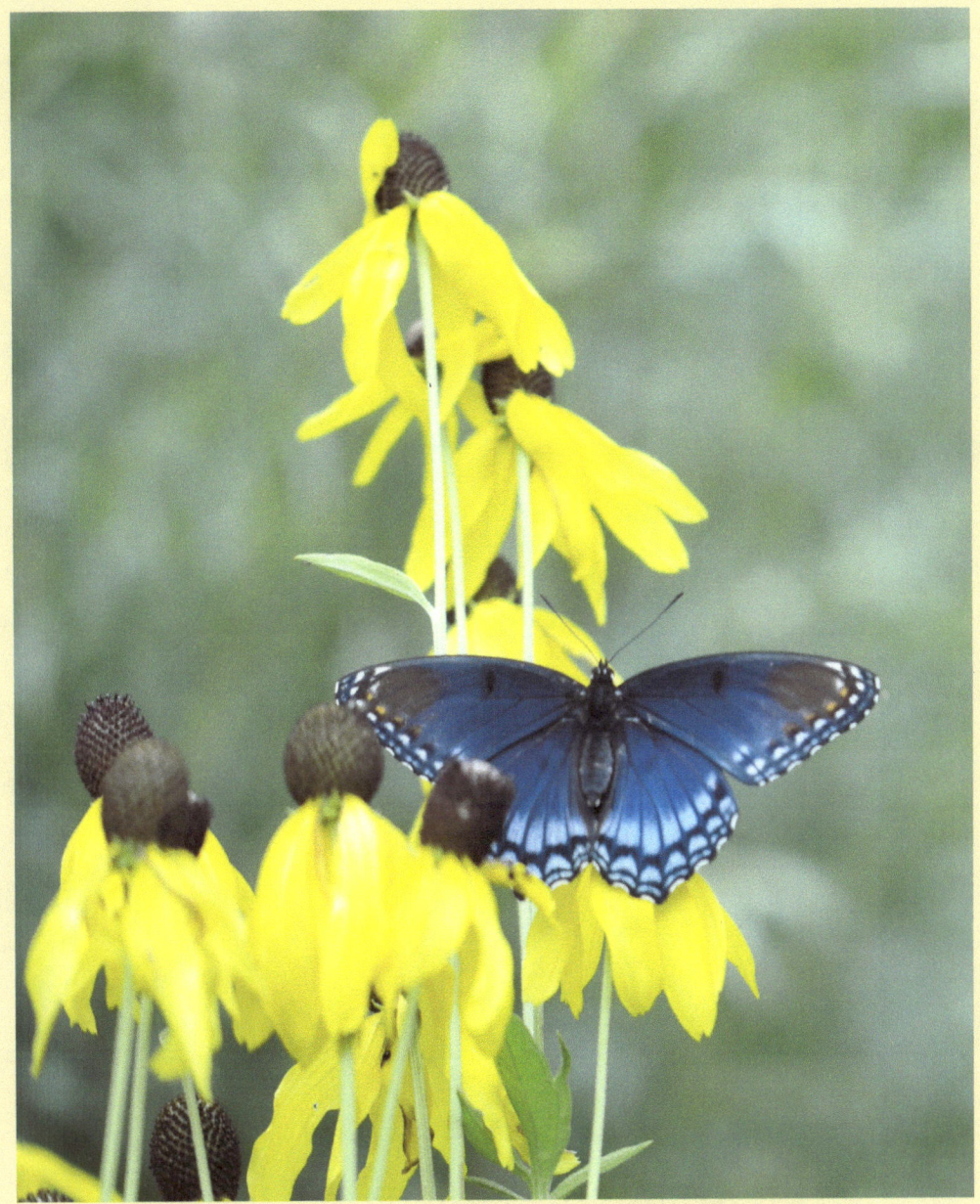

Photographer: Bob Sly
2 acres dedicated to TLC in 1994

Since the Anderson's easement was donated, an additional 300 acres of preserved land have been added to the Powers Creek corridor by TLC through conservation easements and land donations.

Apple Creek Conservation Easement, Woodstock

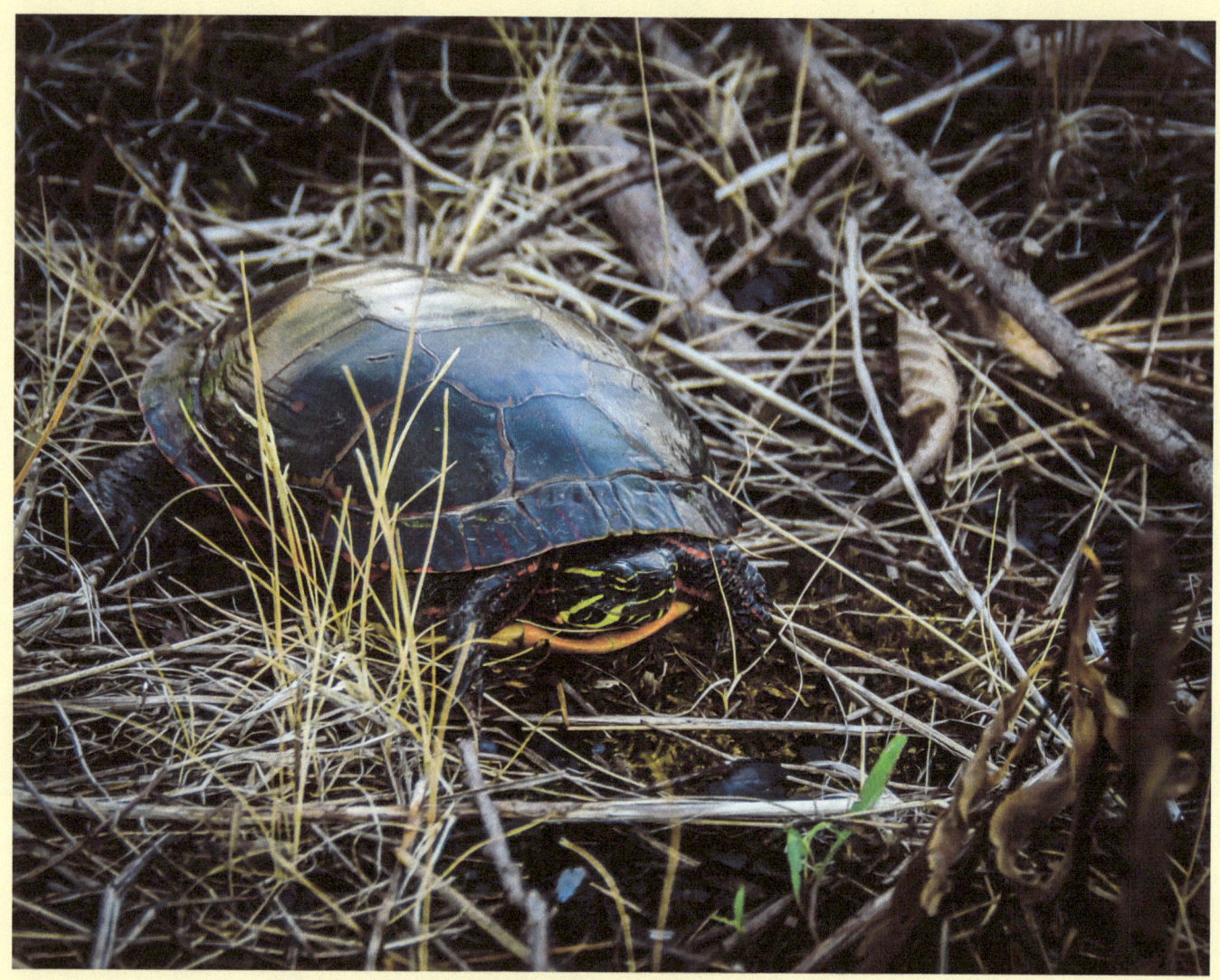

Photographer: Richard Dunn
36.8 acres dedicated to TLC in 2007

Apple Creek is a headwaters stream in the Kishwaukee River system. As the land is
restored, the Conservation Easement will help to ensure that this stream will
provide high quality habitat for a diversity of wetland and upland species.

Bangert Conservation Easement, Alden Township

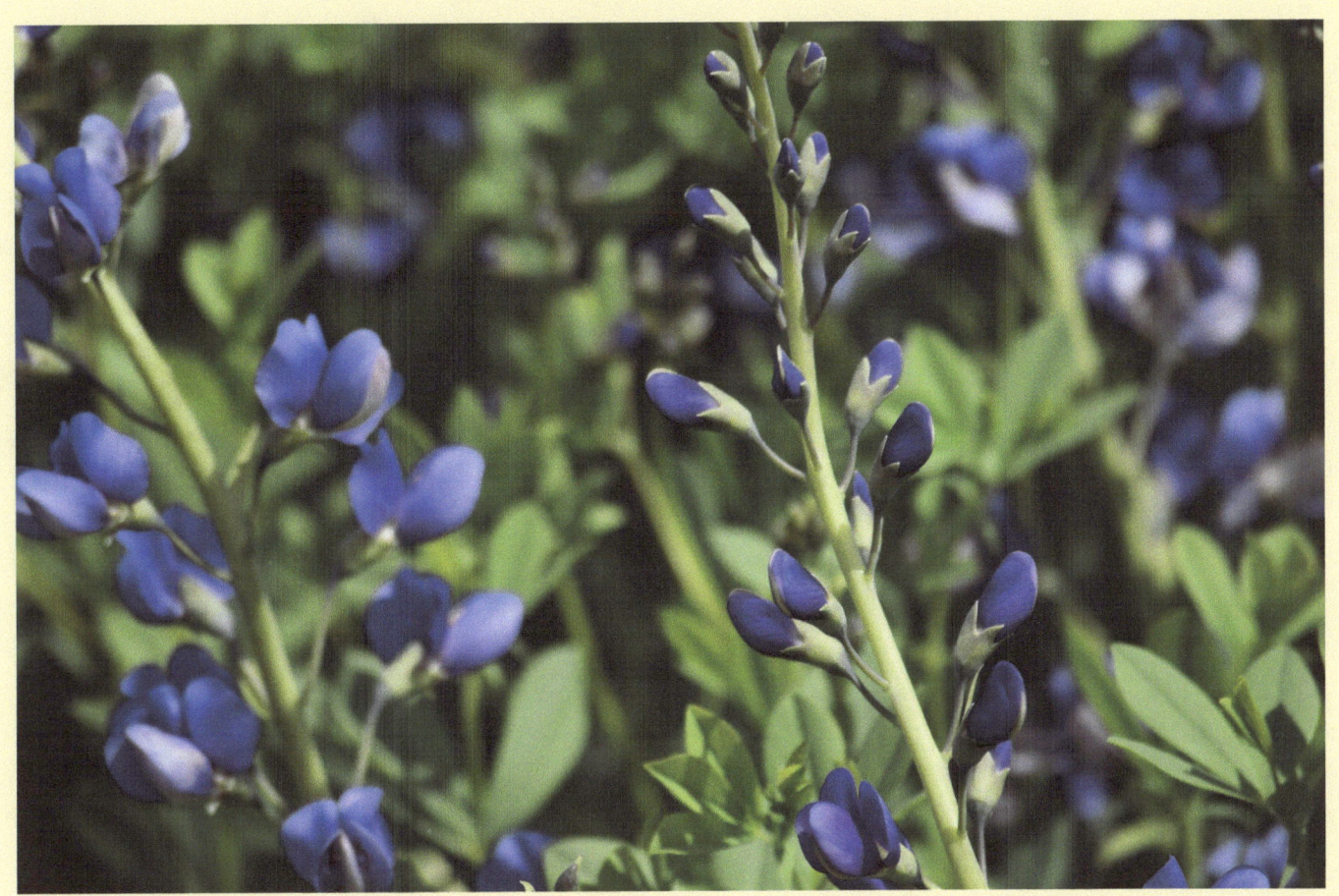

Photographer: Ken Lucas
17 acres dedicated to TLC in 2009

Orrin and Patricia Bangert have been instrumental in conserving the natural areas around the "High Point" in McHenry County (1189 feet above sea level). When they placed a conservation easement on their property, it brought attention to the area and eventually resulted in the Conservation District purchasing 253 neighboring acres.

Crystal Springs Conservation Easement, Nunda Township

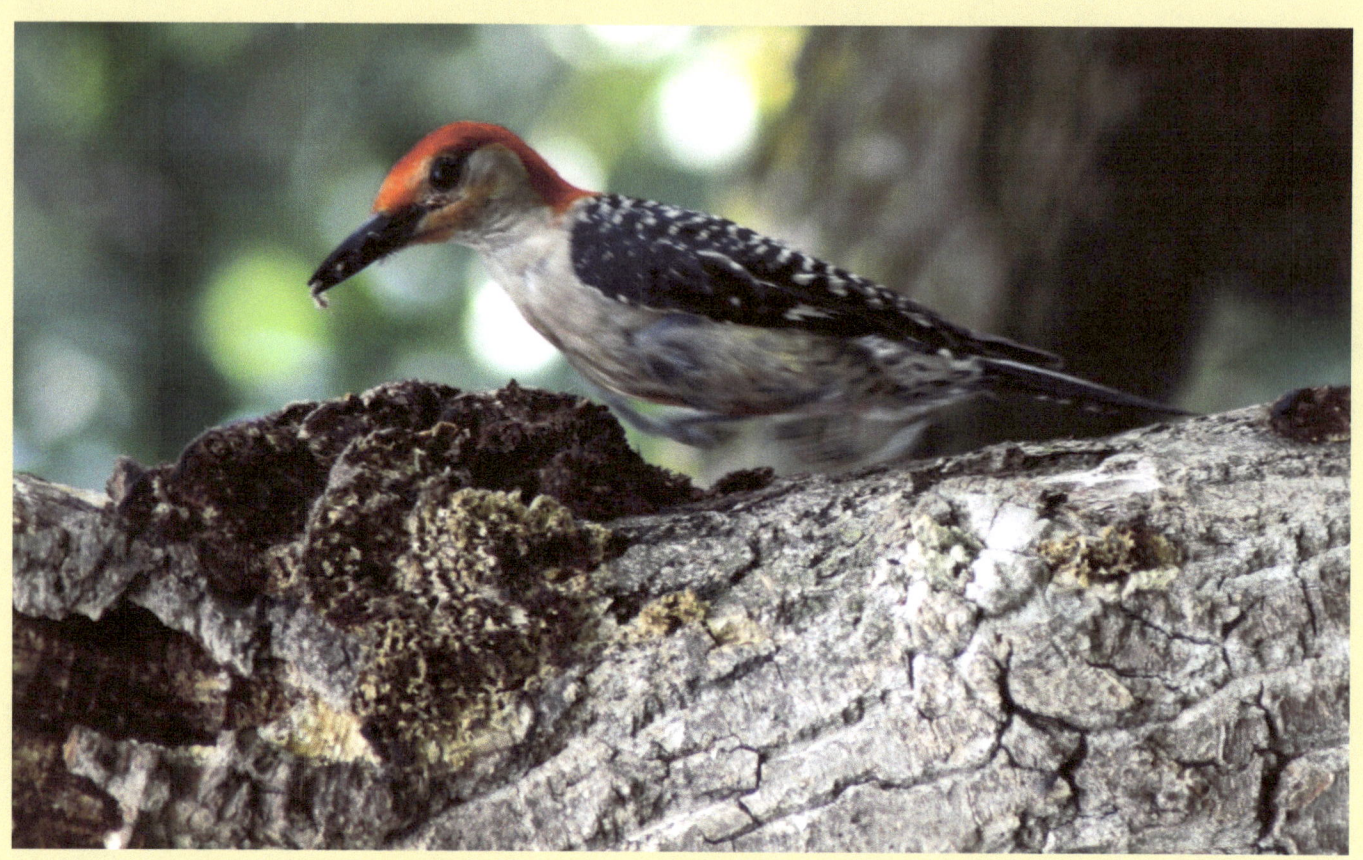

Photographer: Stephanie Liss
250 acres dedicated to TLC in 2006

This huge tract of land dedicated by Sig and Anna Weiler includes a mixture of prairie, wetland, and sporadic massive oaks overlooking farm fields. They have begun efforts to restore this land, and someday there will be 250 acres of wildflowers!

Donato Conservation Area, City of Woodstock

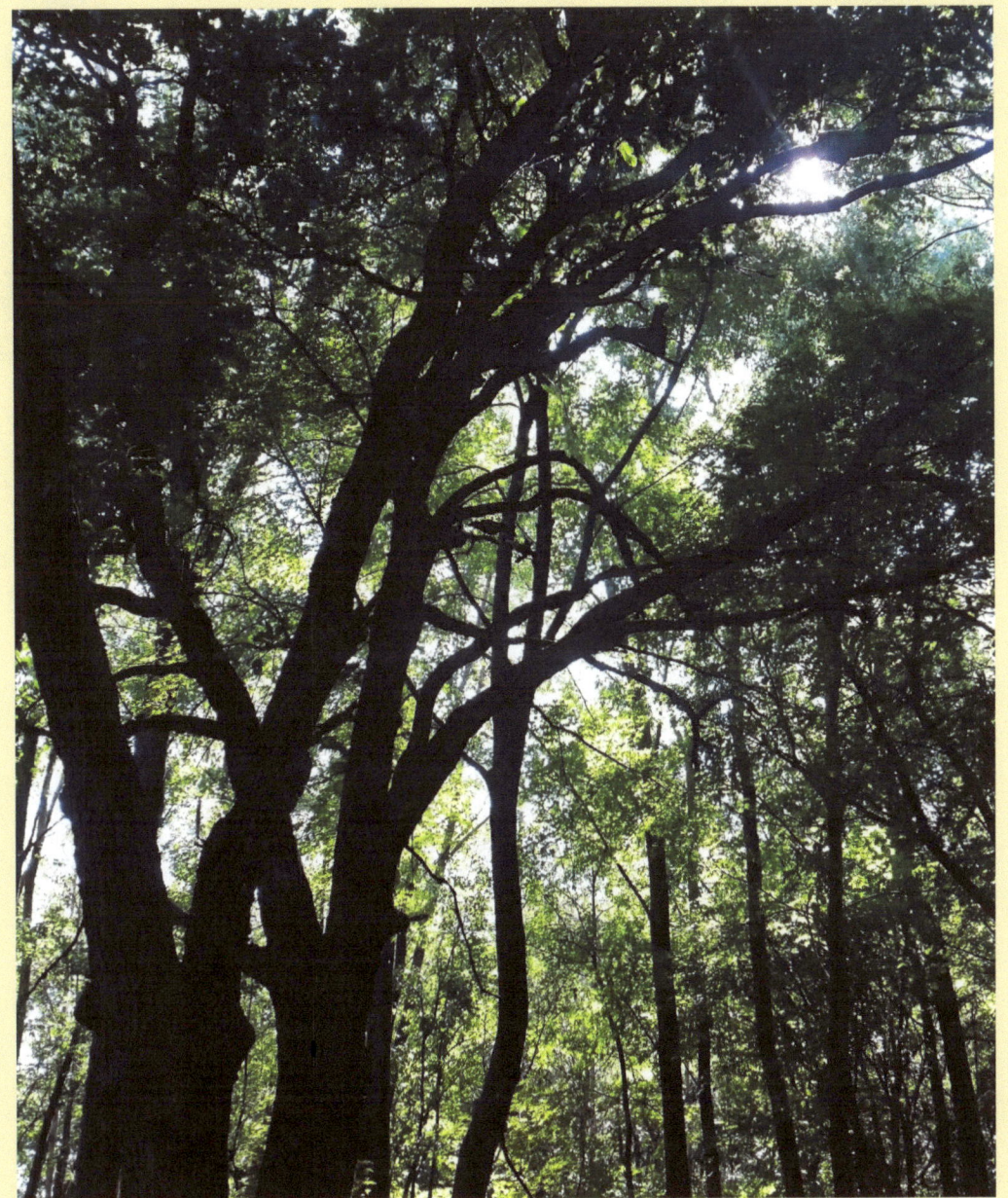

Photographer: Liisa Erita
30 acres managed by TLC since 2006

The restoration efforts here have been championed by the students at Woodstock High School and their teacher Bill Donato. There are volunteer workdays here to remove brush every 1st Sunday of the month during fall and winter if you'd like to lend a hand!

Dutch Creek Conservation Easement, Johnsburg

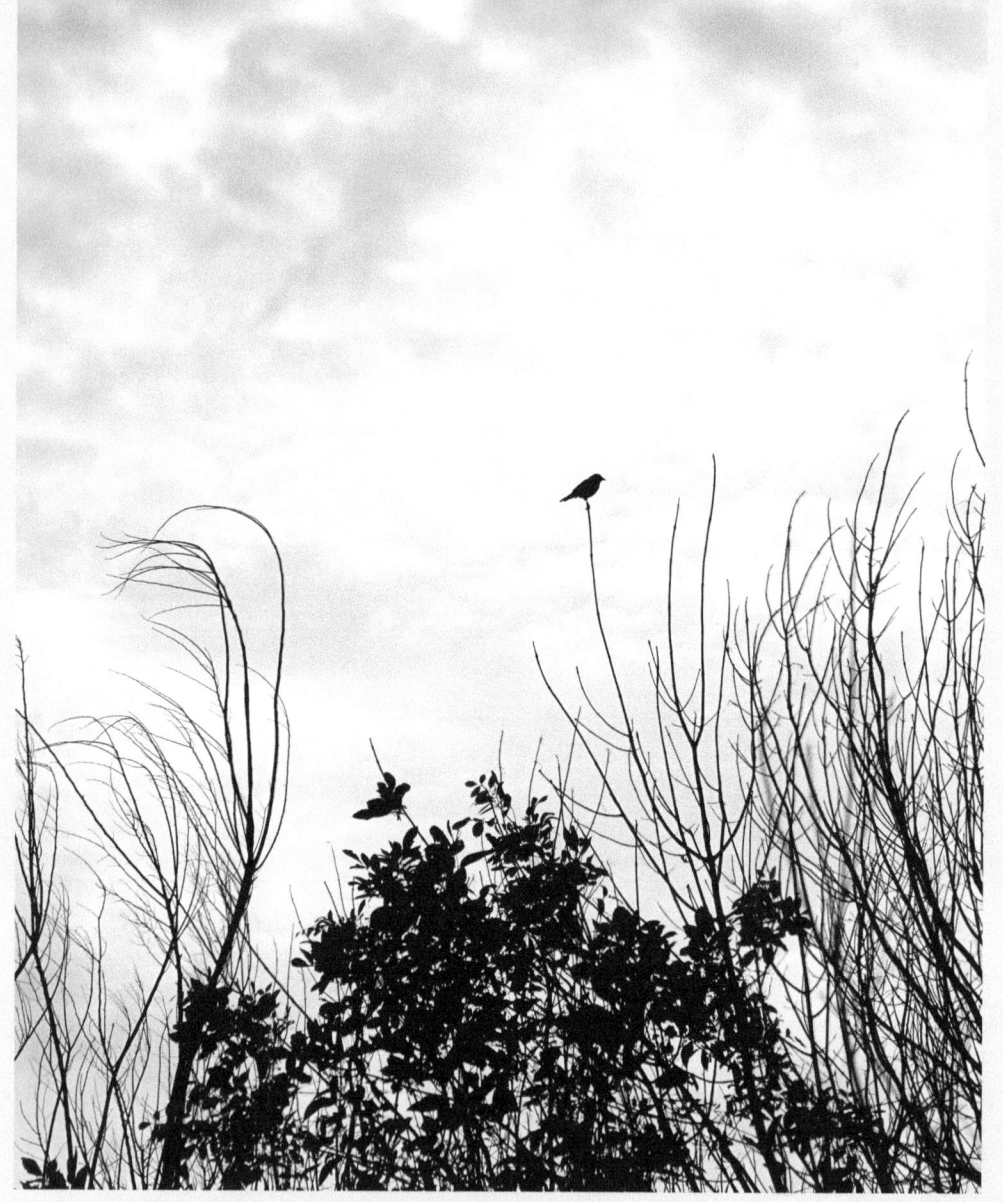

Photographer: Carolyn Flaherty
60 acres dedicated to TLC in 2007

This easement, located within the Dutch Creek Estates subdivision, is part of a larger complex of land protected by TLC, the Conservation District, and the Village of Johnsburg. By working together with other organizations, we can protect the 170 native plant species that call this their home.

Dutch Creek Conservation Easement, Johnsburg

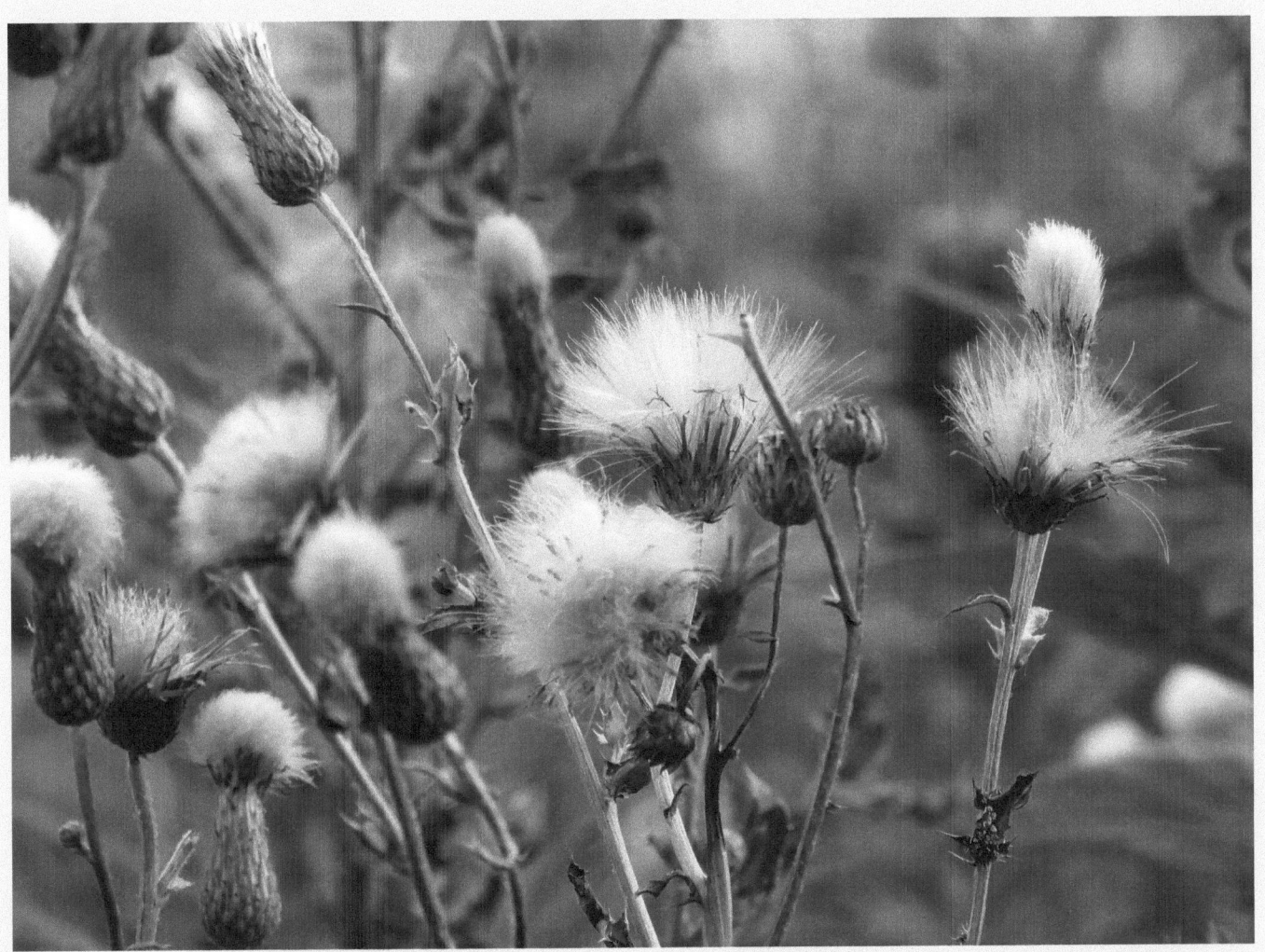

Photographer: Christine Johnson
60 acres dedicated to TLC in 2007

Located here is one of the highest quality headwater streams in the county- Dutch Creek. The stream flows through sedge meadows, fens, and oak woodlands. Students from the local junior high have planted oaks each Arbor Day for the past six years – over 250 oaks in 6 years!

Frisbie Conservation Easement, Hartland Township

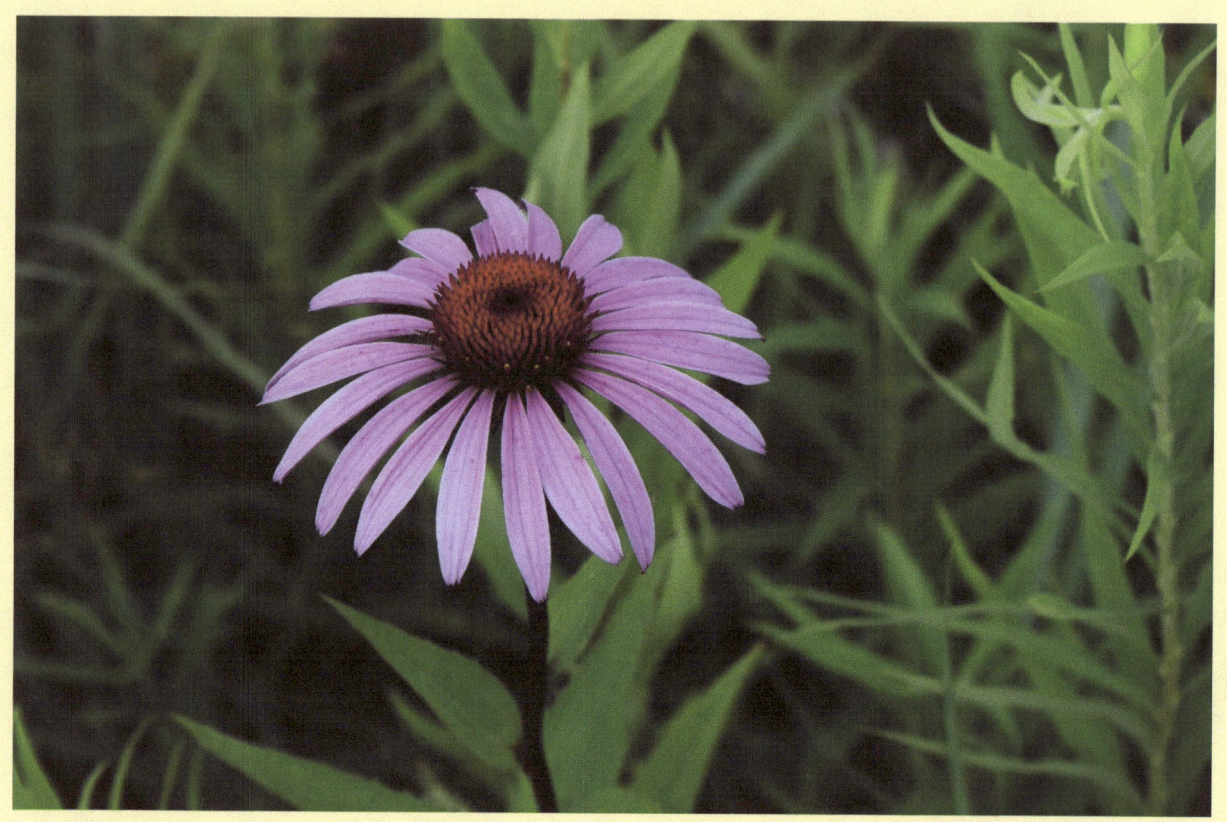

Photographer: Penny Martin
56 acres dedicated to TLC in 2011

When this land was purchased by Marlene and Hugh Frisbie in 1993 it was mostly farmland. Now meadows of prairie, wetland, and woodland wildflowers and grasses spread out across the land.

Hennen Conservation Area, City of Woodstock

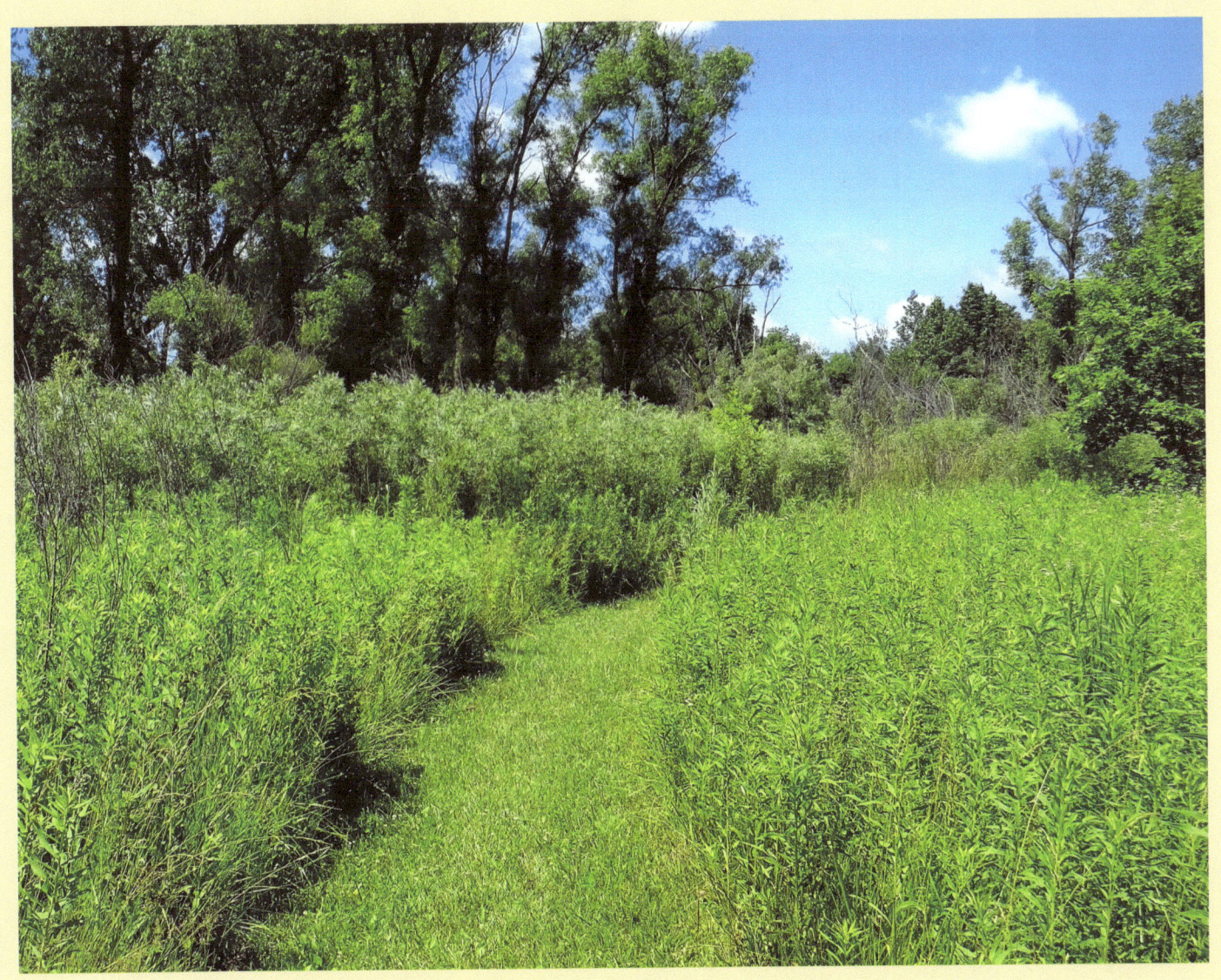

Photographer: Reg Kennedy
25 acres dedicated to TLC in 2008

Phyllis and Tony Hennen acquired this land in the early 70s, planting thousands of native hardwood seedlings. They donated the land to the city of Woodstock as a public park, and TLC moved their offices to the farmhouse. Ongoing restoration of the property continues, and we're proud to continue what the Hennens began.

Hidden Marsh Conservation Easement, Hebron Township

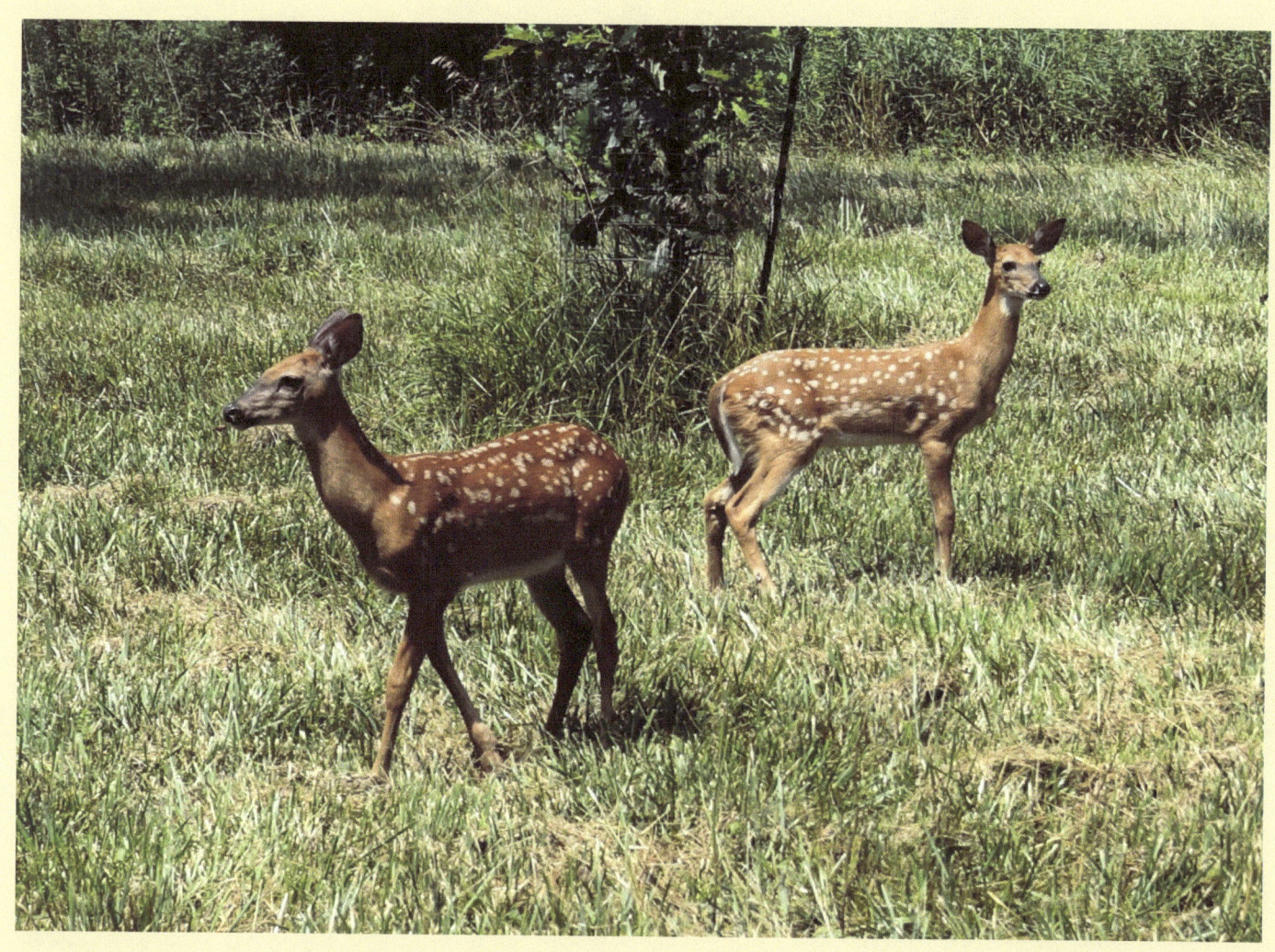

Photographer: Rob Peterson
25 acres dedicated to TLC in 2008

Two glacial kames will never be mined for gravel. A sedge meadow will never be filled for development. An oak woodland will never be cleared for a farm field. This is the power of a conservation easement.

Hidden Marsh Conservation Easement, Hebron Township

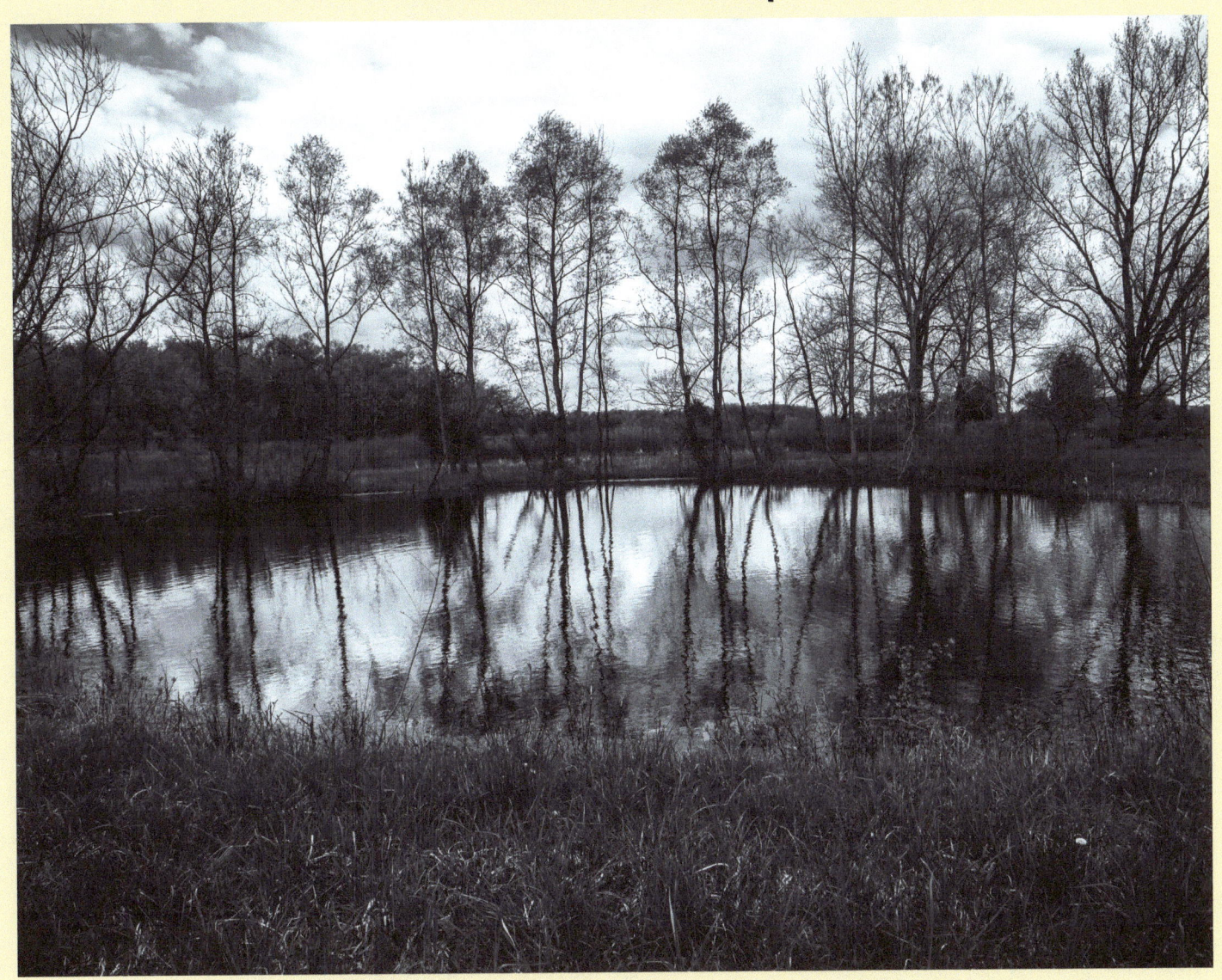

Photographer: Kate McGuire
25 acres dedicated to TLC in 2008

When David and Joanne first purchased their land, there was so much buckthorn and honeysuckle that it was hard to see the kame, the wetland, and even Wisconsin (just across the property line). They have put countless hours of brush clearing, burning, and adding seed. The young oak trees will thank them every day for the next couple hundred years.

Hidden Marsh Conservation Easement, Hebron Township

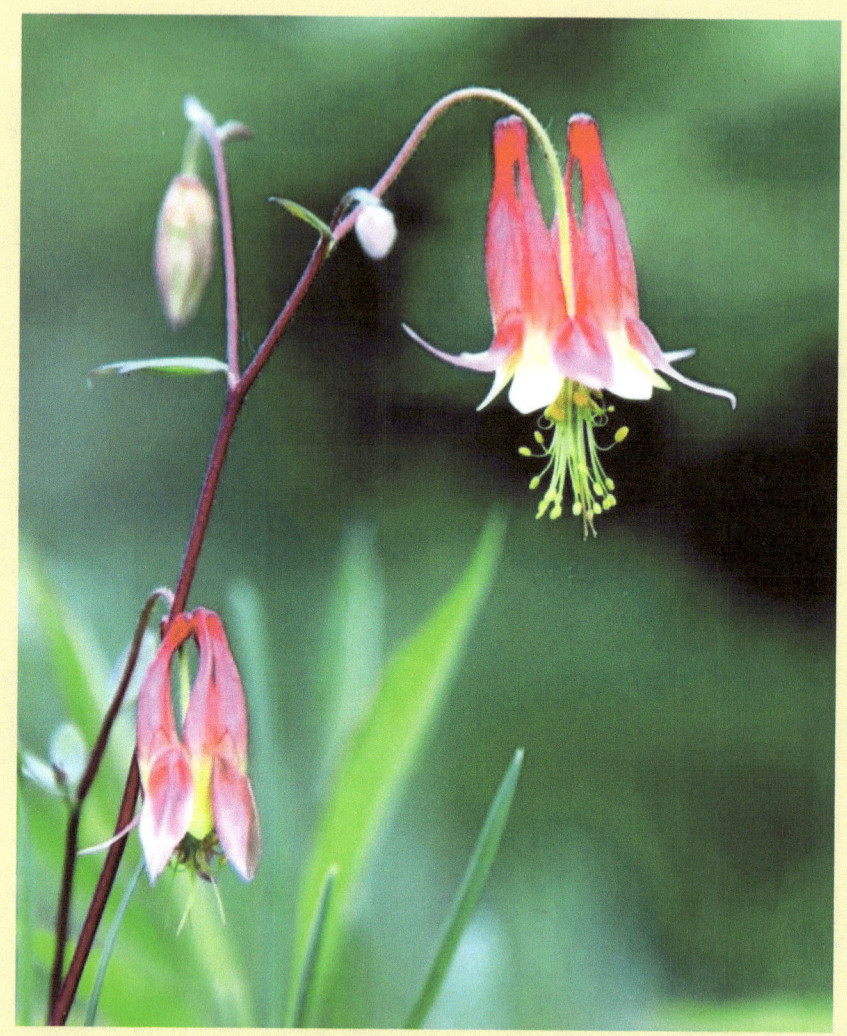

Photographer: James Schroeder
25 acres dedicated in 2007

Rare glacial landforms exist on this property- a few small kames and one large esker. Standing on top of these will let you find a few remnant dry gravel hill prairie plants, and also gives an excellent overview of the whole property.

Horsefair Springs Fen Conservation Easement, Village of Spring Grove

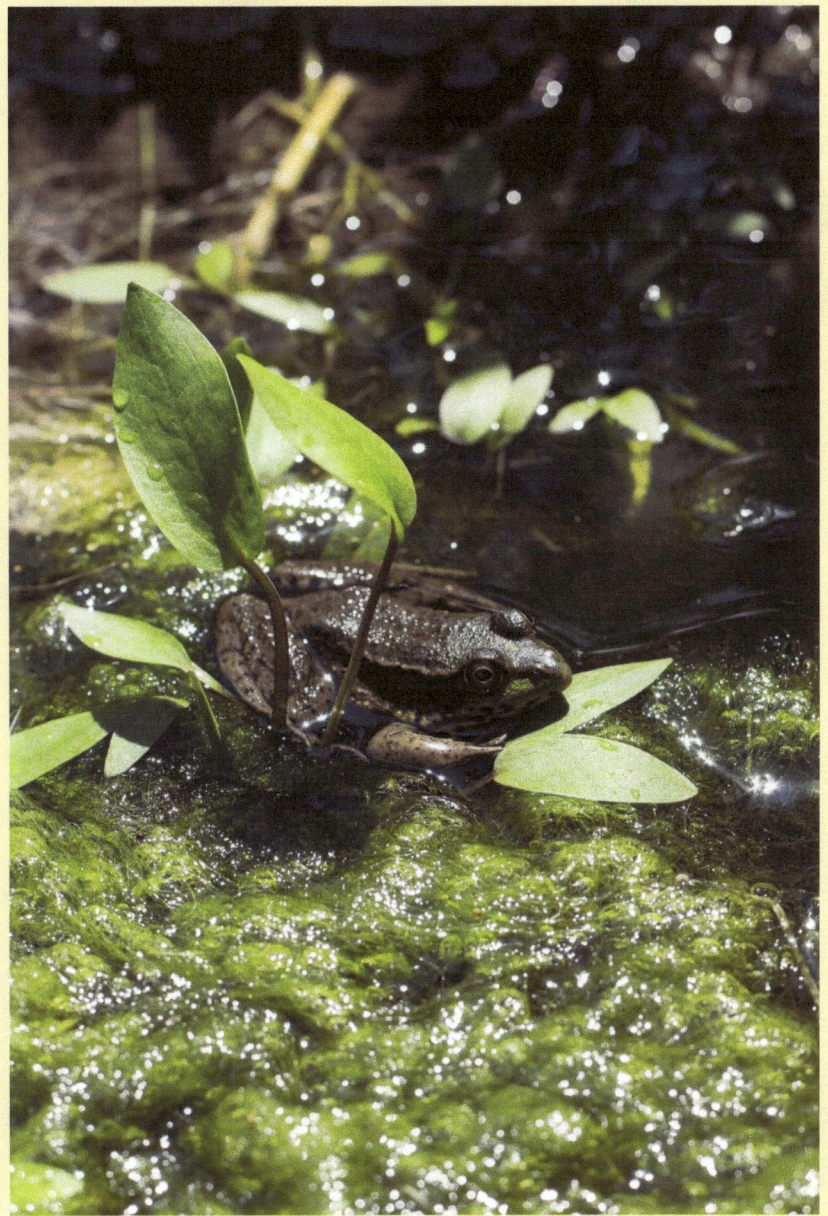

Photographer: Marissa Floress

9 acres dedicated to TLC in 2006

This easement is part of one of the largest, highest quality unprotected wetlands in the county. Located next to the Thousand Oaks subdivision, the easement provides a nice pocket of nature for all the residents, so they can appreciate the oak trees and various prairie flowers right in their back yards.

Kaskel Conservation Easement, Hebron Township

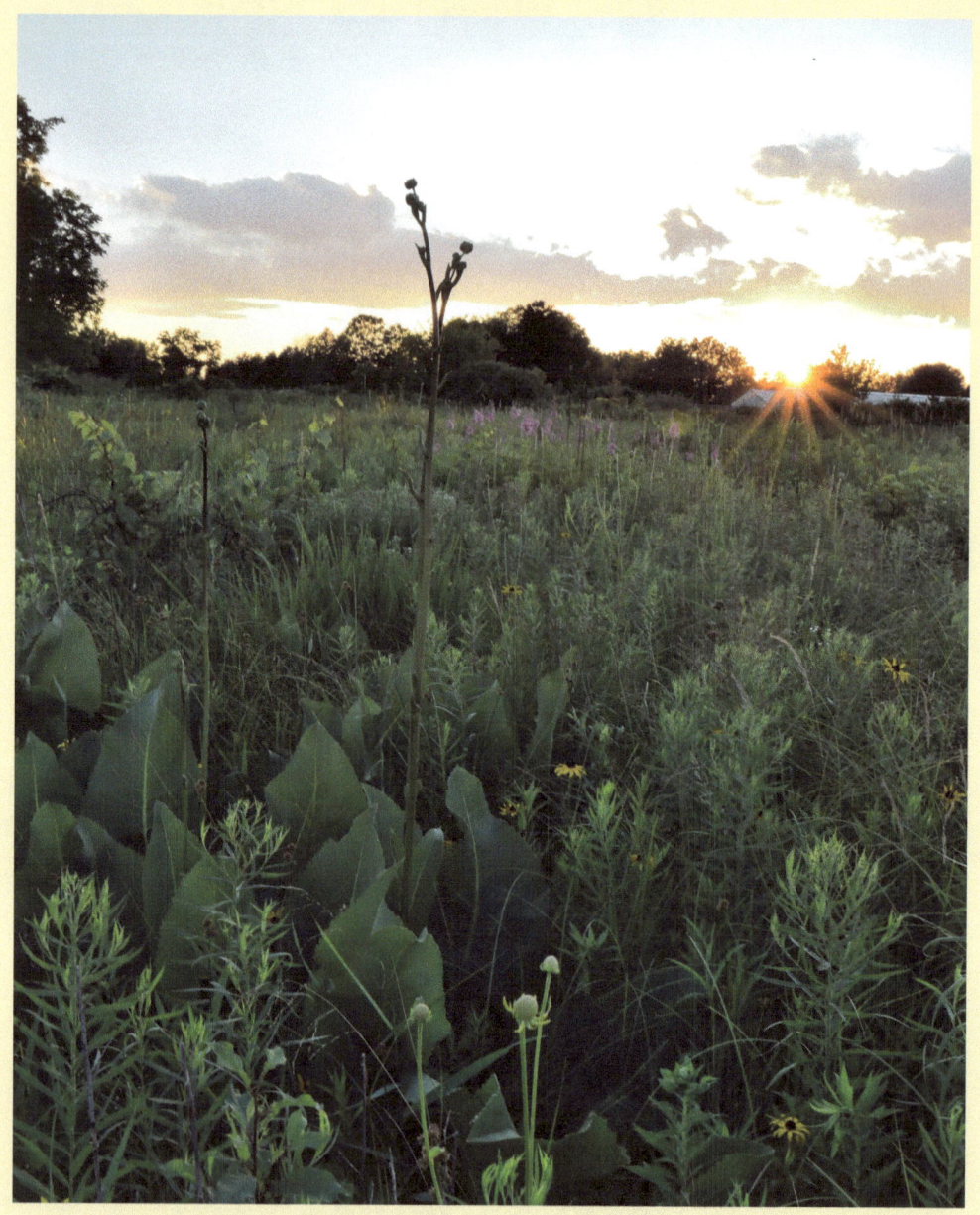

Photographer: David Hankins
15 acres dedicated to TLC in 2004

The Kaskel property is one of the highest quality sedge meadow and wet prairie habitats remaining in the county. Owners Jack and Maurine Kaskel of Red Buffalo Nursery have done an amazing job taking care of this natural area.

Lynda Clayton Preserve, Johnsburg

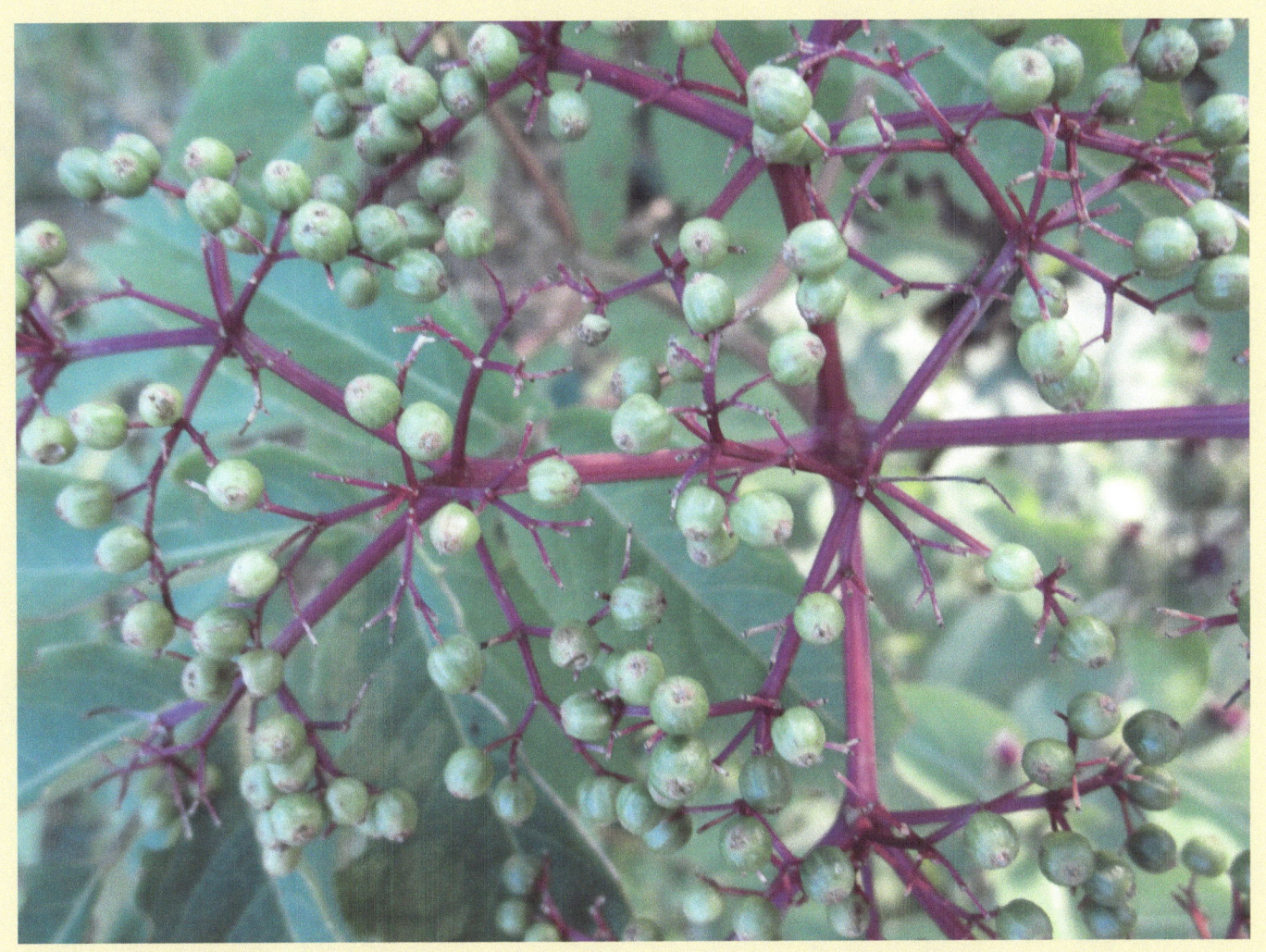

Photographer: Mary Jo Stedman
12 acres donated to TLC in 2013

This property has a diversity of ecosystems and habitat. Most of the land is a nice sedge meadow and creek corridor, which abounds with flowers, sedges, and ferns throughout the year. Upland areas on the northern half of the site have some wonderful large oak trees.

Moehling Conservation Easement, Dorr Township
Third Place

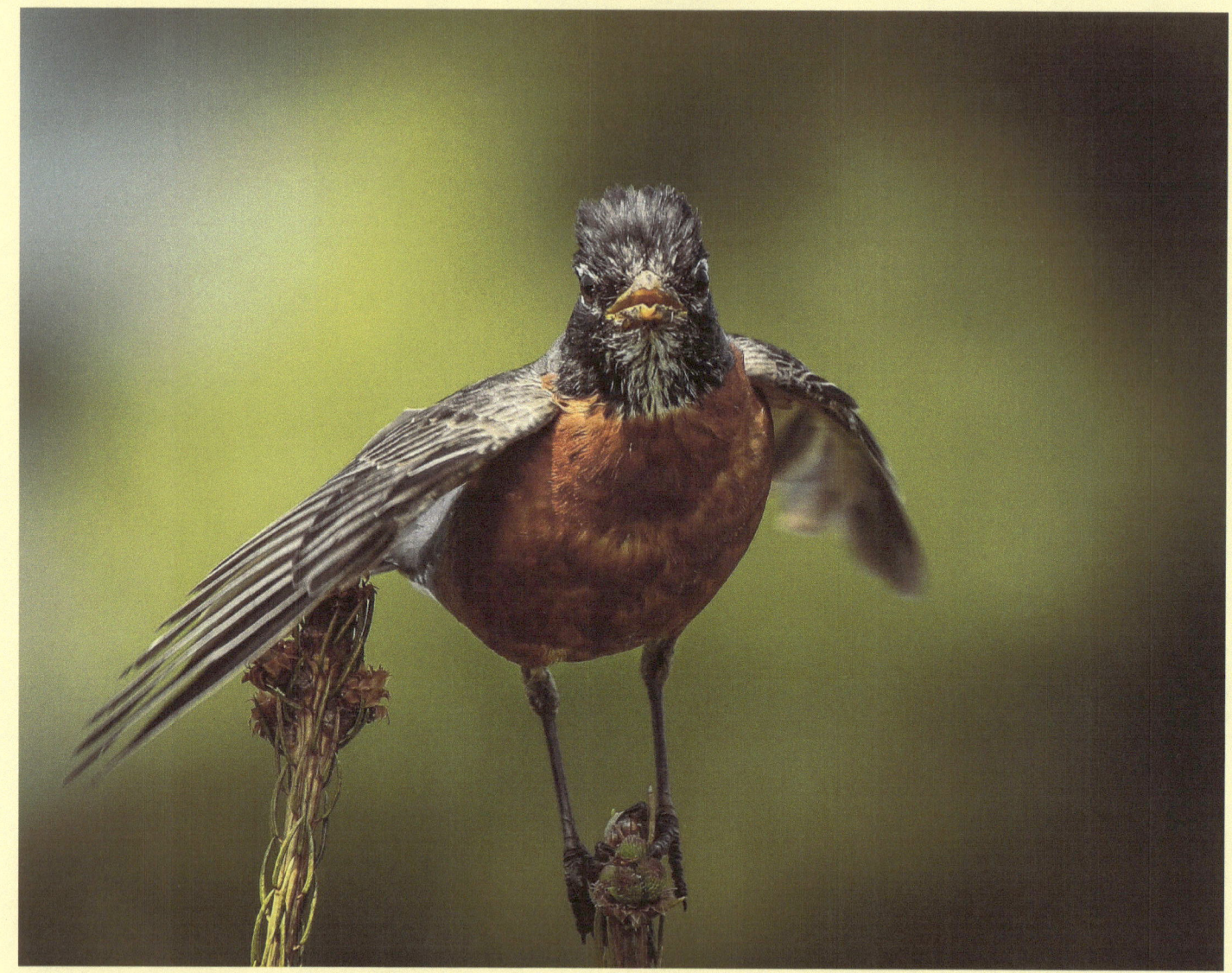

Photographer: Cynthia Lawler
15 acres dedicated to TLC in 2010

Mel and Cheri Moehling protected their remnant oak hickory woods, and also preserved the scenic vista and natural beauty with a permanent conservation easement. The property is also adjacent to the Queensbury Farm Conservation Easement, expanding the protected natural areas.

Moehling Conservation Easement, Dorr Township

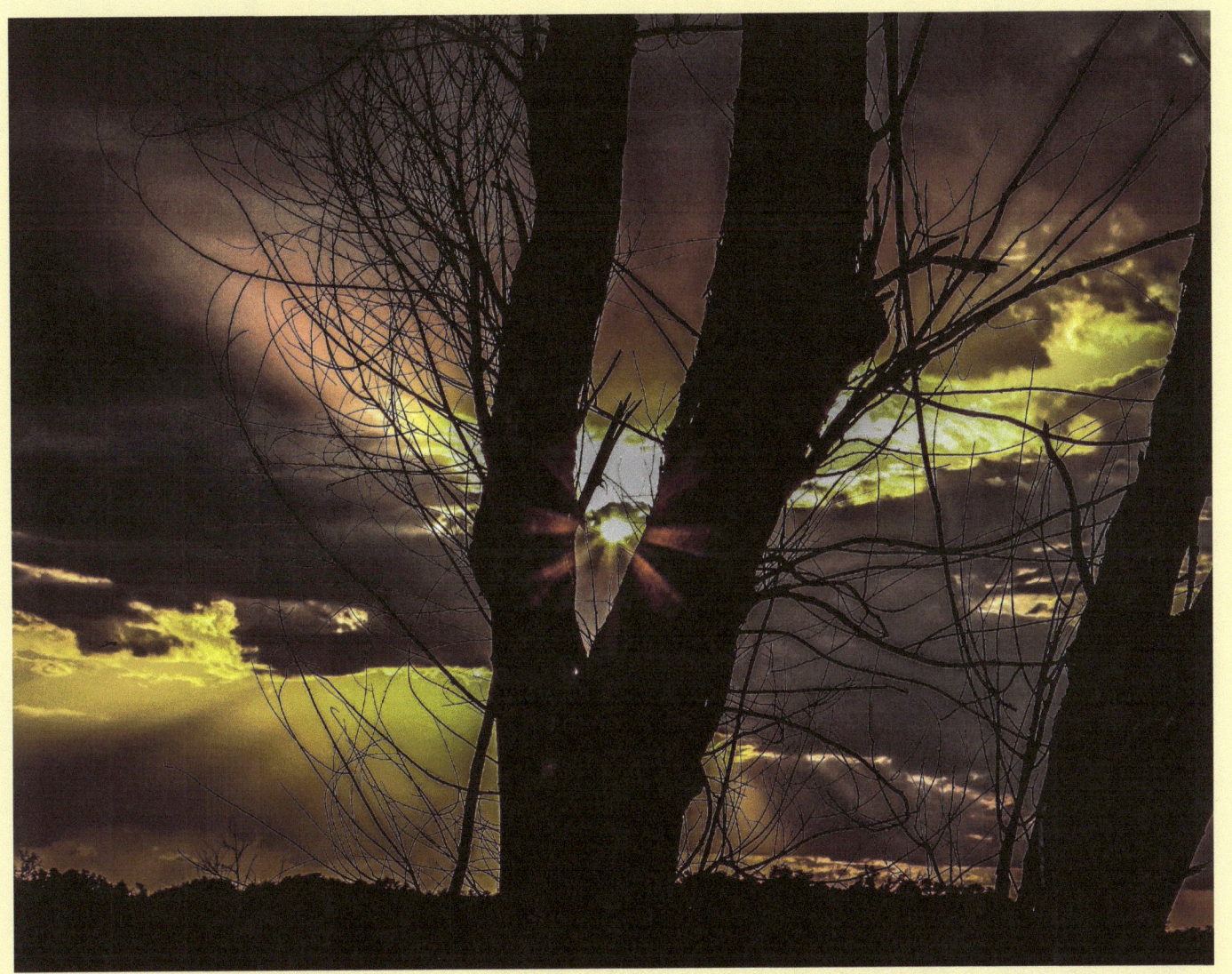

Photographer: Cynthia Lawler
15 acres dedicated to TLC in 2010

This property boasts remnant oak/hickory woods, wetlands, and a mix of trees planted through the Forest Management Plan of Illinois. Mel and Cheri have been busy clearing invasive brush and planting wildflowers, and every year the place gets more beautiful!

Pensinger Conservation Easement, Dorr Township

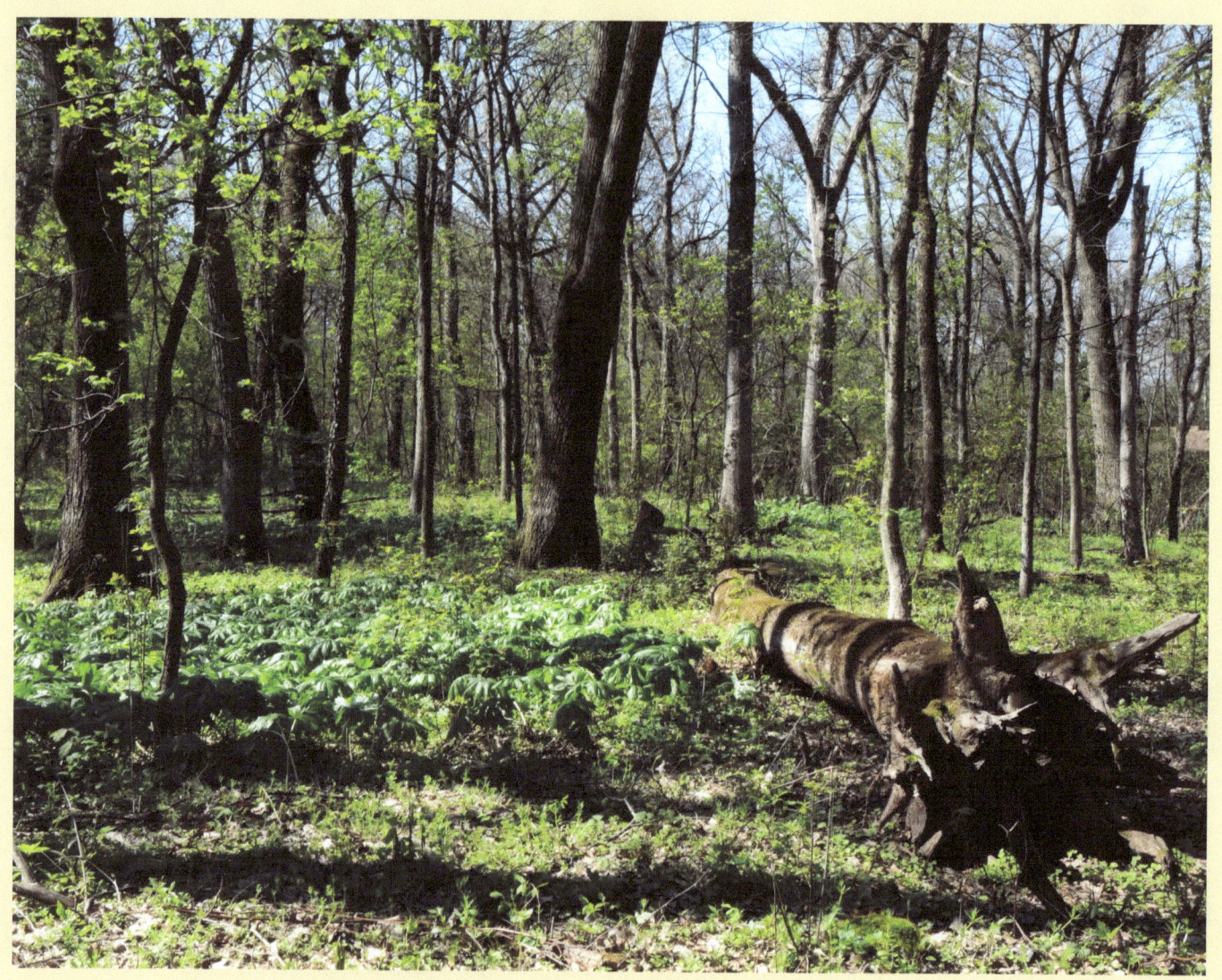

Photographer: Linda Gurgone
3 acres dedicated to TLC in 2009

Lynn and Ray Pensinger protected their grove of old hickory and oak trees with a permanent easement. Since then, they've been clearing the invasive honeysuckle and buckthorn from beneath the oaks. With the increase in light, an abundance of wildflowers have spring up on the woodland floor.

Pistakee Conservation Area, McHenry Township

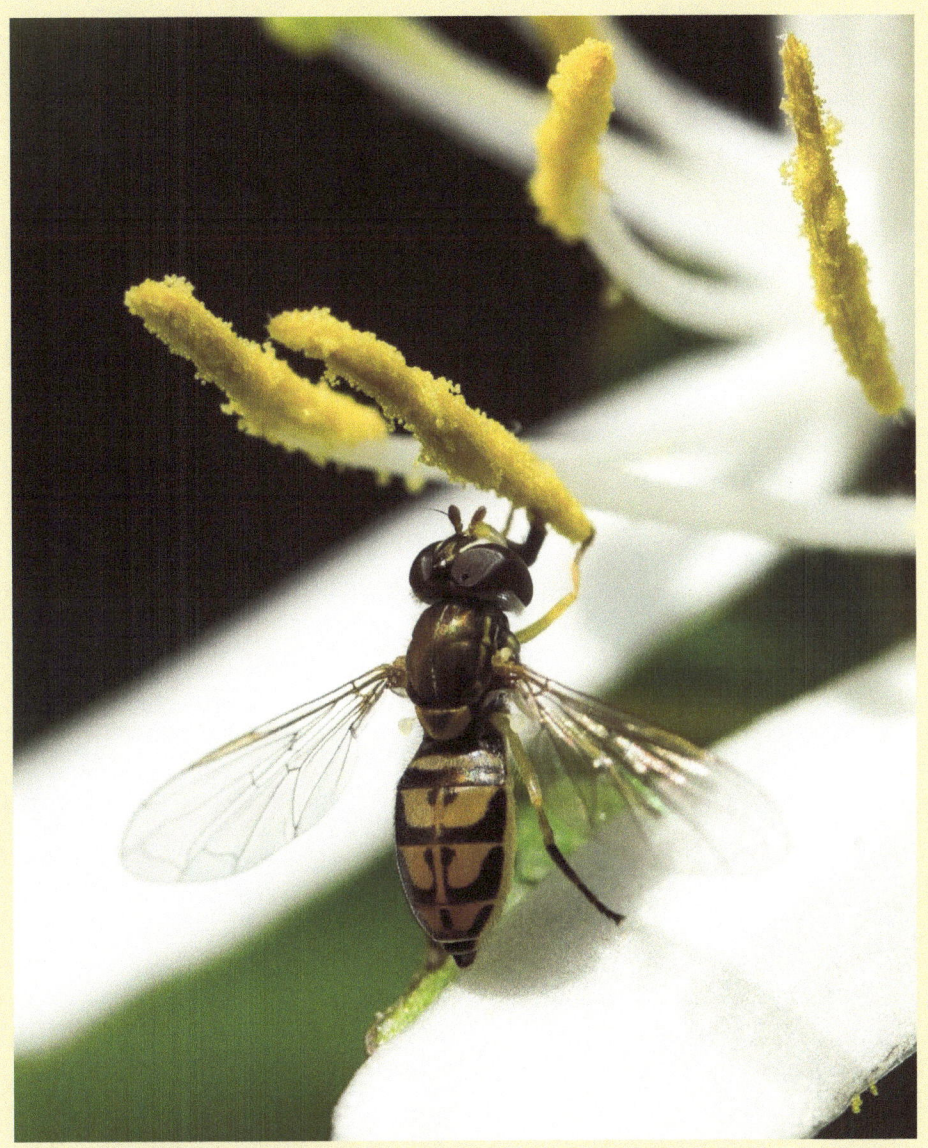

Photographer: Julie Boatright
3 acres donated to TLC in 2009

This land along Pistakee Lake has been in the same family since the 1800s. The three Olson sisters agreed on a donation to TLC, protecting the natural lakeshore and a lagoon in an area where mowed lawns line most of the lake.

Powers Creek Conservation Area, Nunda Township

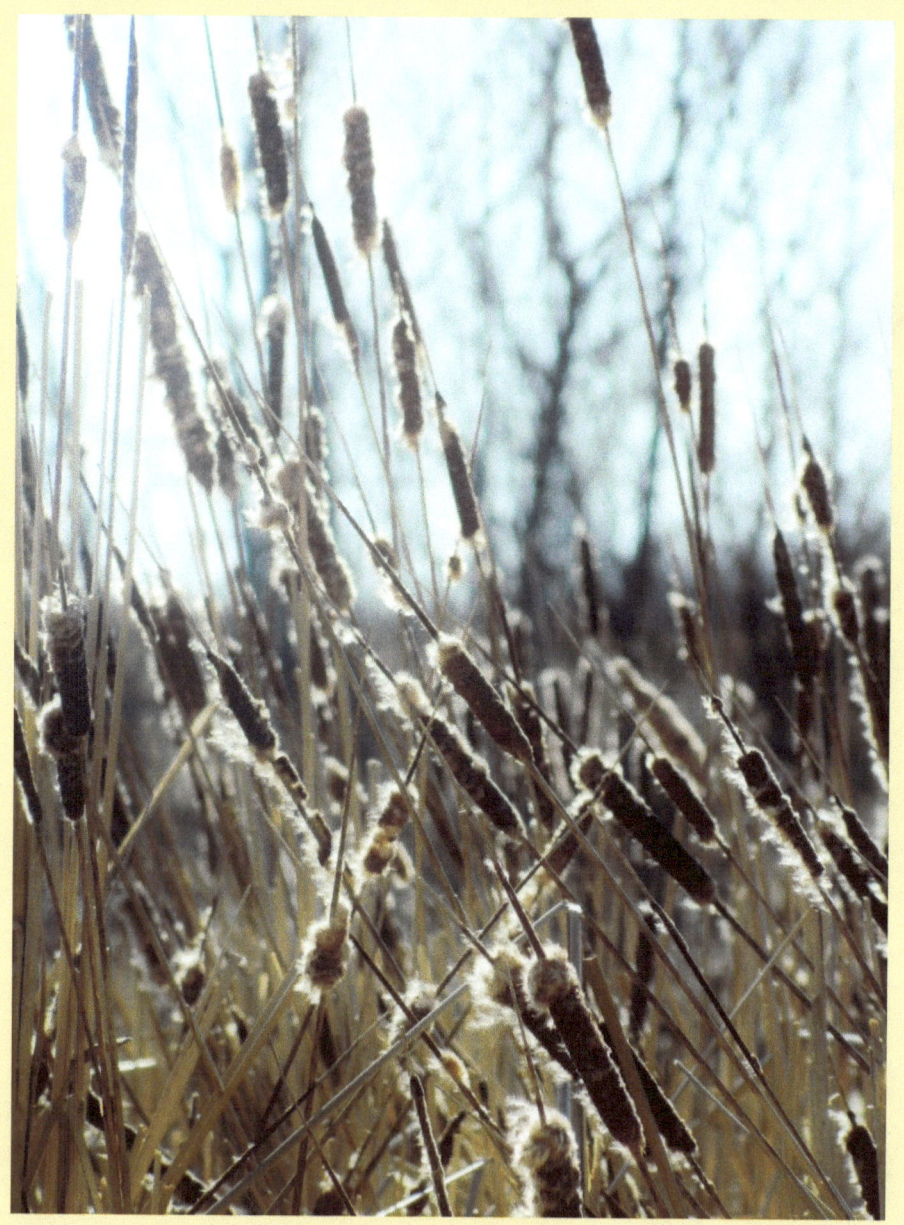

Photographer: Diana Floress
22 acres donated to TLC in 2002

Powers Creek was a sod farm before TLC acquired it and started holding volunteer workdays. By removing drain tiles, adding native seed and taking out invasive species like buckthorn, the property has become a natural gem.

Prairie Ridge Conservation Area, City of Woodstock

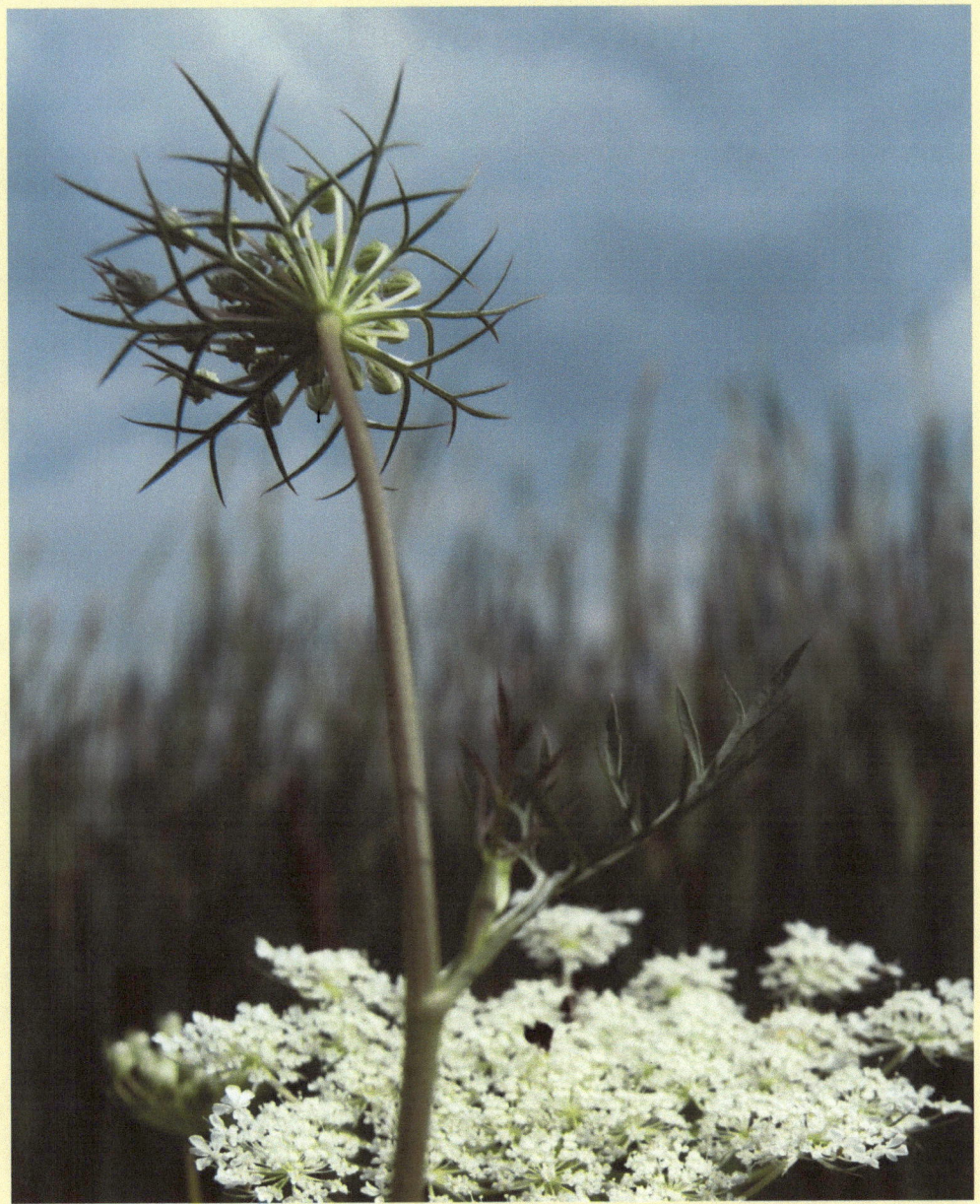

Photographer: Maureen Larson
9 acres dedicated to TLC in 1996

Prairie Ridge Fen was a tangle of buckthorn and reed canary grass in 1996 when TLC was granted a conservation easement and long-term management agreement by the owner, the City of Woodstock. Today it is a living testament to the power of restoration, harboring uncommon species like turtlehead and the Baltimore Checkerspot butterfly!

Reiland-Van Bussum Conservation Easement, Nunda Township

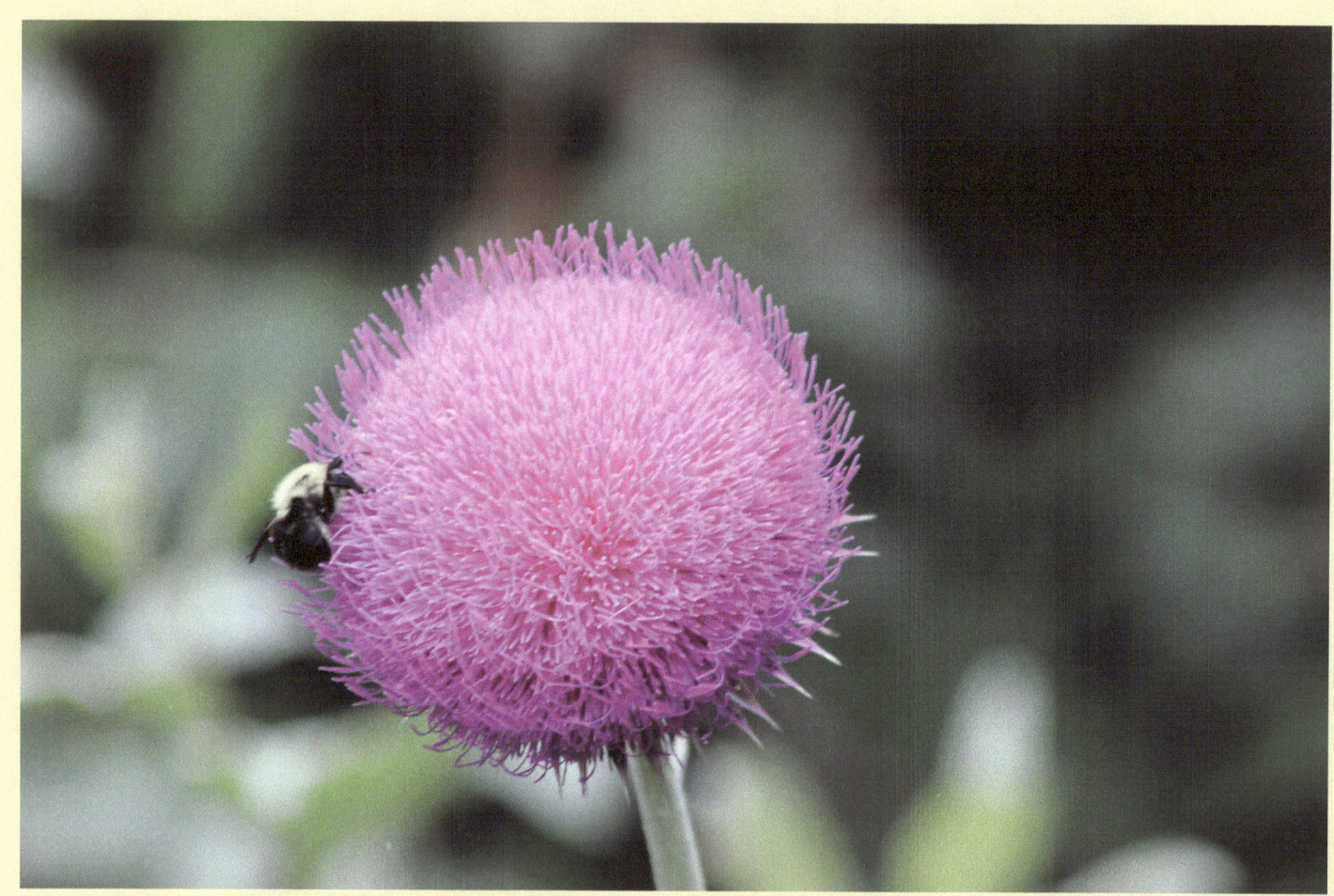

Photographer: Rich Pawlacki
17 acres dedicated to TLC in 2006 and 2015

After a neighbor donated a 4 acre parcel to TLC, Kathy Reiland dedicated a 14 1/2 acre conservation easement protecting the entirety of this beaver-created wetland indefinitely. In 2015, she enlarged the easement by 2 1/2 acres!

Ryders Woods Conservation Area, City of Woodstock
First Place

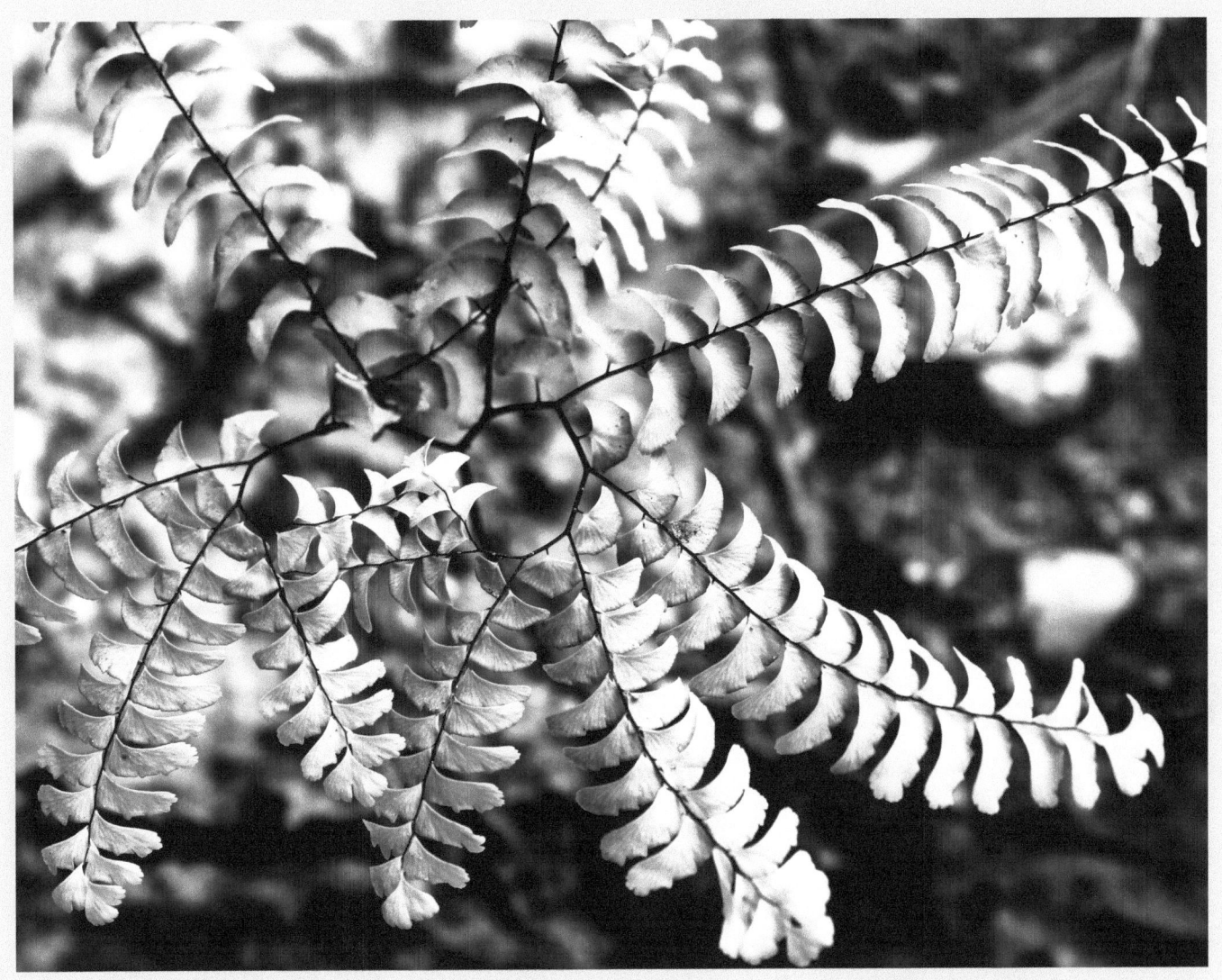

Photographer: Narayani Hiffman
23 acres managed by TLC since 2006

There was a group called "Friends of Ryders Woods" active back in the 1970s who worked to ensure this gem located blocks from the Woodstock Square would provide peaceful enjoyment to residents forever. Today, the City of Woodstock, TLC, and local volunteers work together to maintain the woods.

Ryders Woods Conservation Area, City of Woodstock

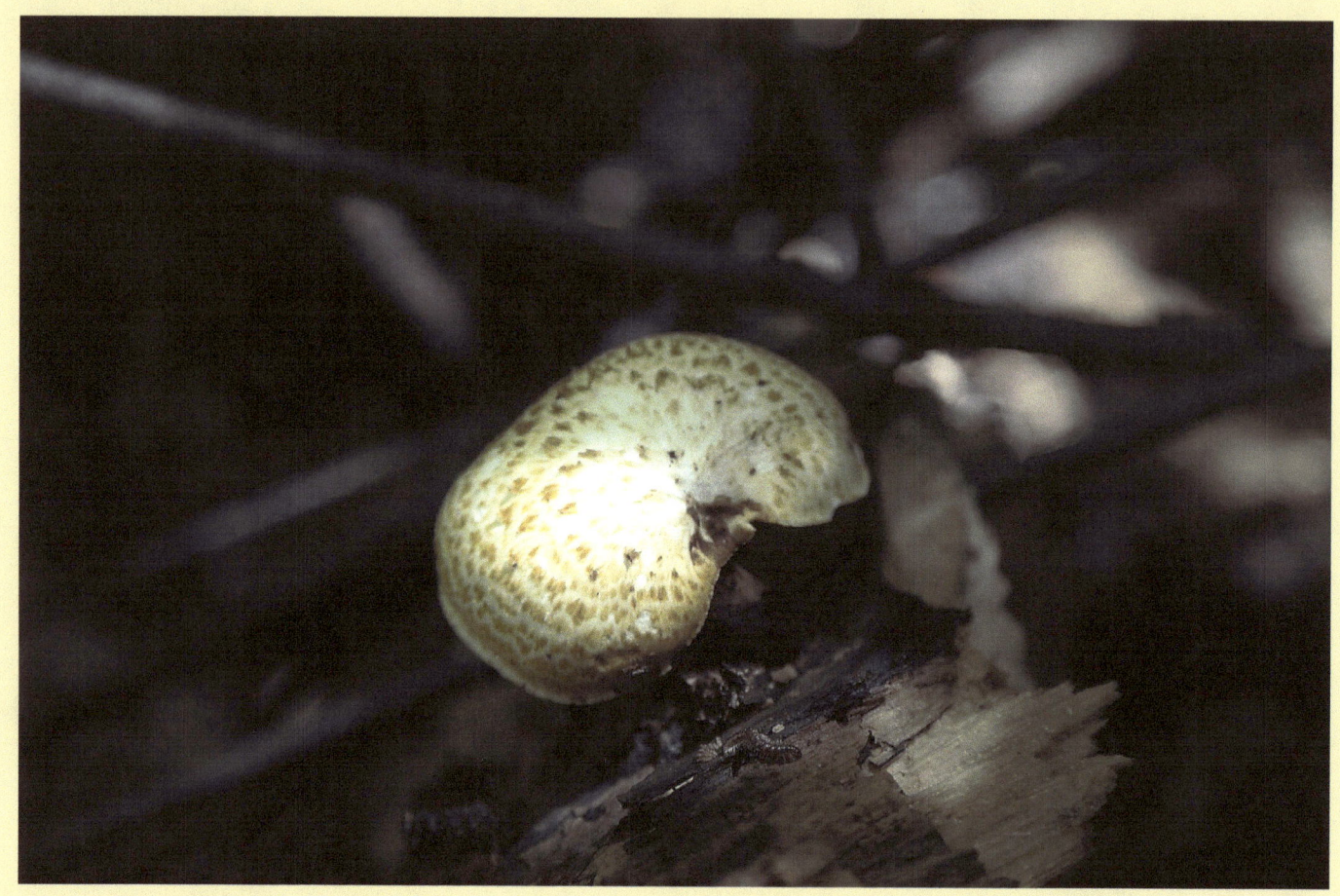

Photographer: Nicole Domanico
23 acres managed by TLC since 2006

By managing the buckthorn and other invasive species, TLC and volunteers have transformed the woods into an open and inviting sanctuary for people and wildlife.

Soulful Prairie Conservation Easement, Hartland Township - Second Place

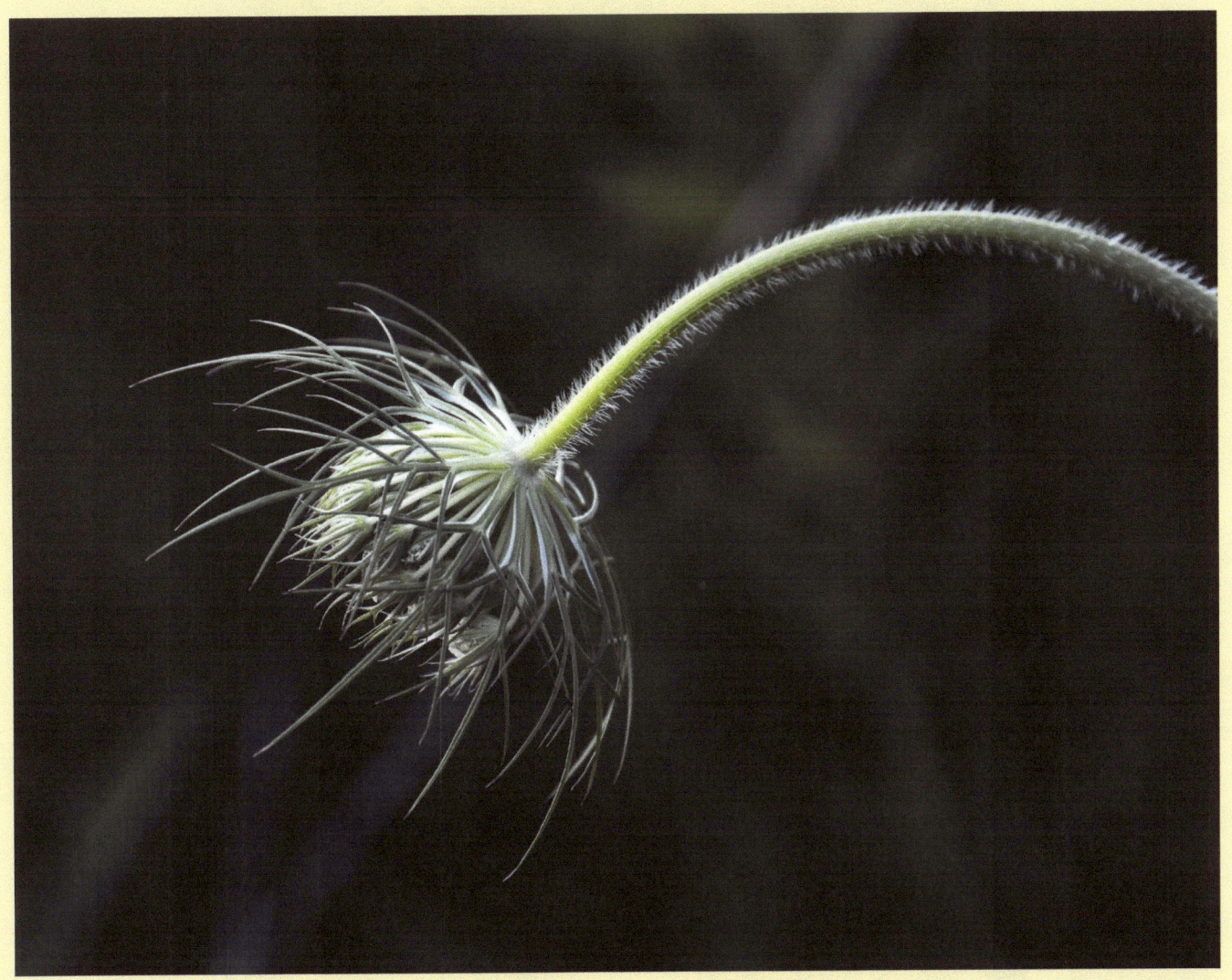

Photographer: Margie Bjorkman
33 acres dedicated to TLC in 2013

The wetlands and ponds found on this property serve as a resting and feeding place for migratory birds, especially waterfowl and shorebirds. The marsh attracted a great diversity of wildlife, including birds of concern such as the yellow-headed blackbird and the least bittern.

Soulful Prairie Conservation Easement, Hartland Township

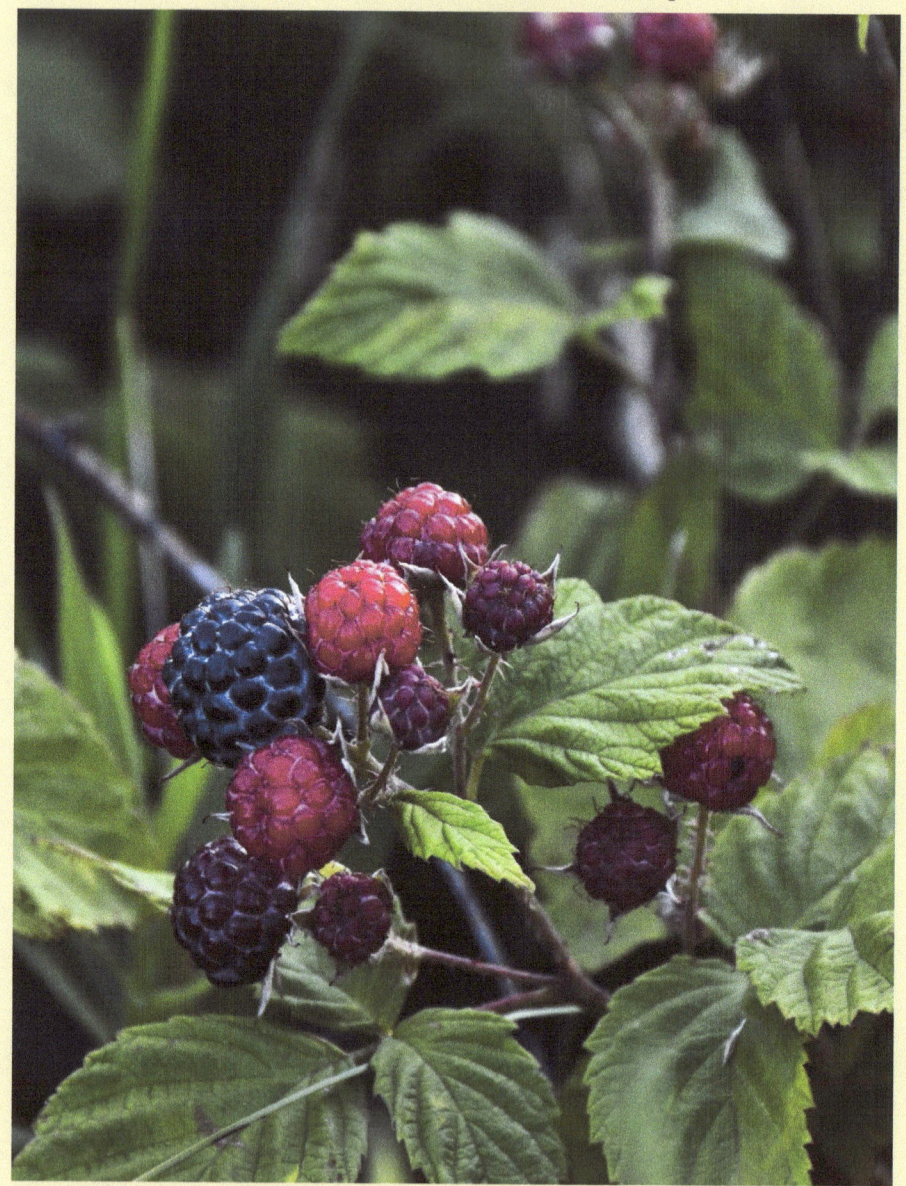

Photographer: Margie Bjorkman
33 acres dedicated to TLC in 2013

In the words of landowner Linda Bruce, "The focus was to create a beautiful place with sustainability, restoration and salvage in mind. Each step along the path has brought about growth and change. As we restore the land there is a sense of renewal that we wish nothing more than to share with others."

Spring Hollow Conservation Easement, Bull Valley
Honorable Mention

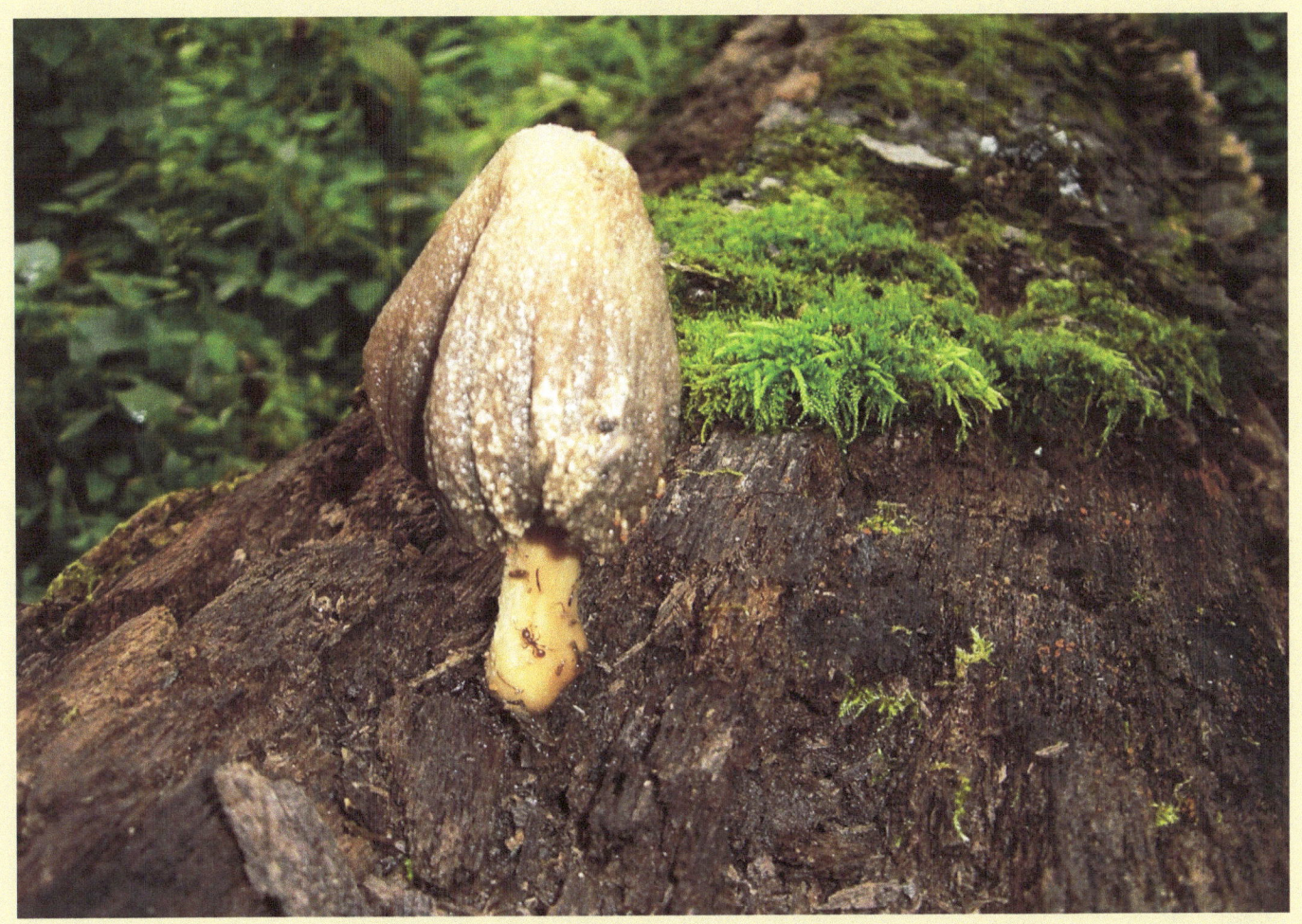

Photographer: Kendal Stephens
25 acres dedicated in 1977, transferred to TLC in 2013

Dick and Betty Babcock were the first Illinois family to dedicate a permanent conservation easement on their land in December 1977, making use of the law which Dick Babcock helped create. They named this place Spring Hollow for its many natural springs and rolling topography, and it is still in the family today.

Spring Hollow Conservation Easement, Bull Valley

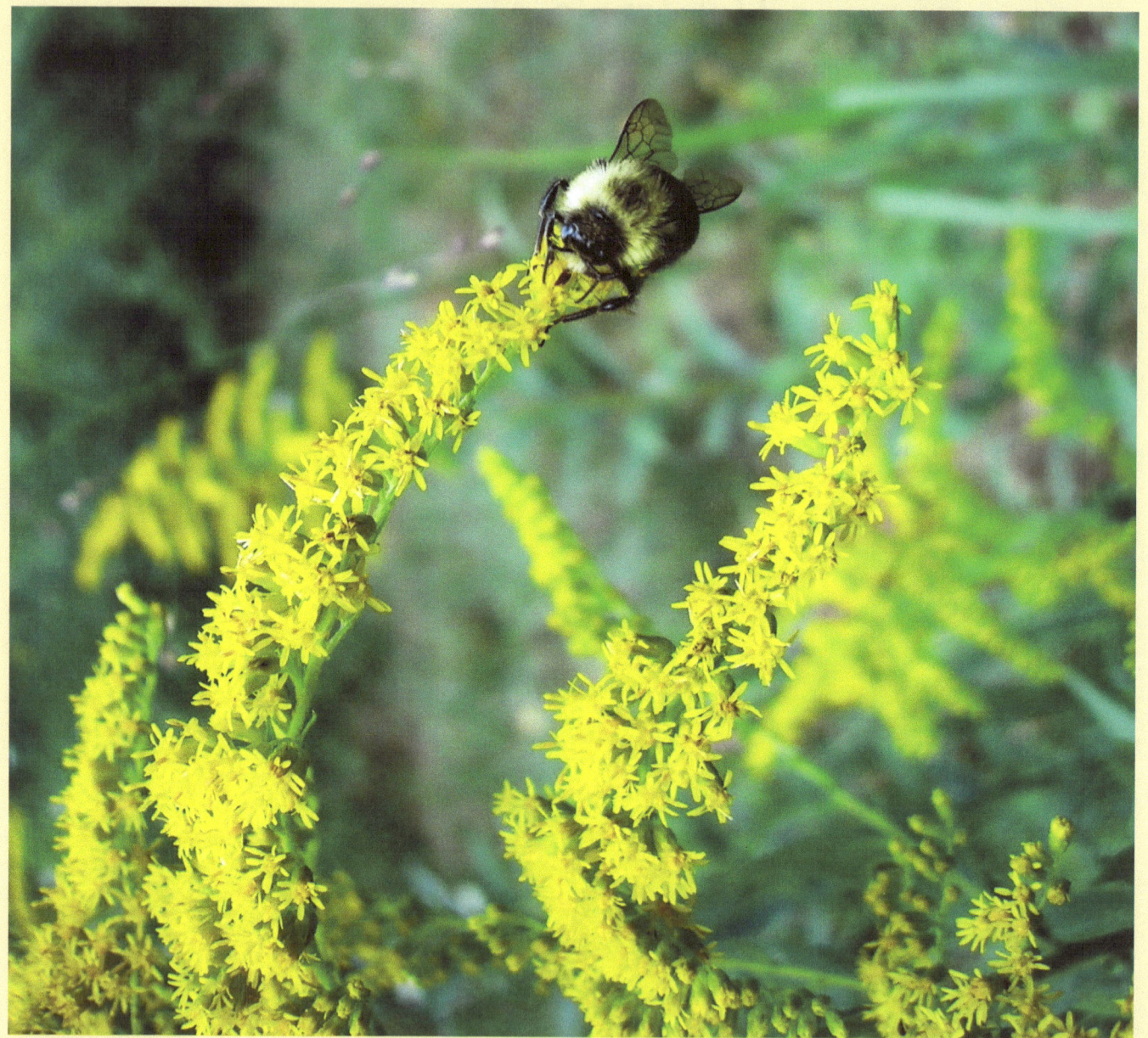

Photographer: Kendal Stephens
25 acres dedicated in 1977, transferred to TLC in 2013

This easement has achieved Illinois Nature Preserve Status- a classification given to the highest quality remaining habitats in Illinois. Today it is still being managed by the daughter of the original easement grantor, and it looks great!

Stowe Conservation Easement, Alden Township
People's Choice, Friday

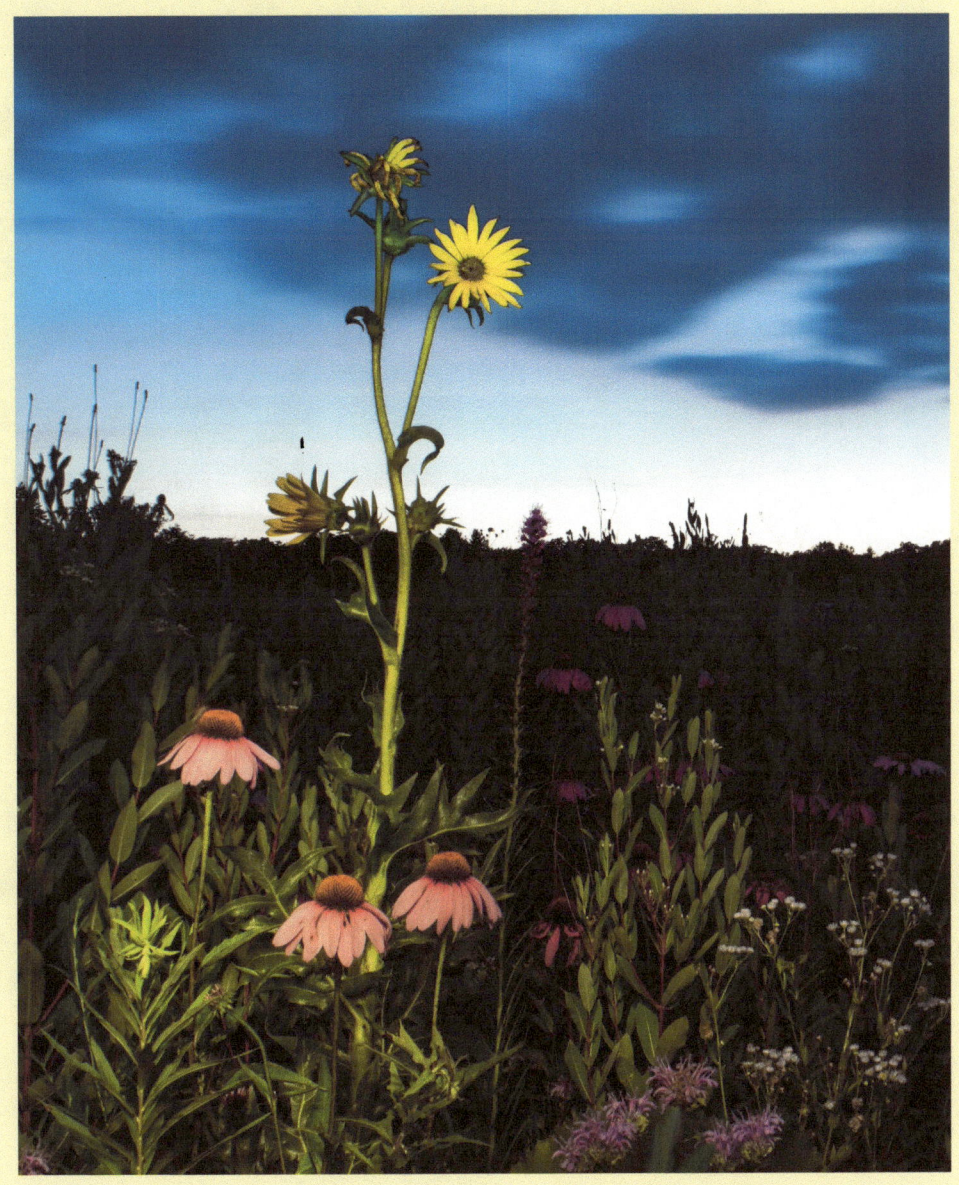

Photographer: John Weaver
1.5 acres dedicated to TLC in 2008

Randy and Karen Stowe have worked hard to preserve the land over the years, not only on their own property but also in the area of the highest glaciated point in Illinois. The commitment of the Stowes and their neighbors resulted in MCCD's purchase of the High Point Conservation Area!

Tagatz Conservation Easement, Bull Valley

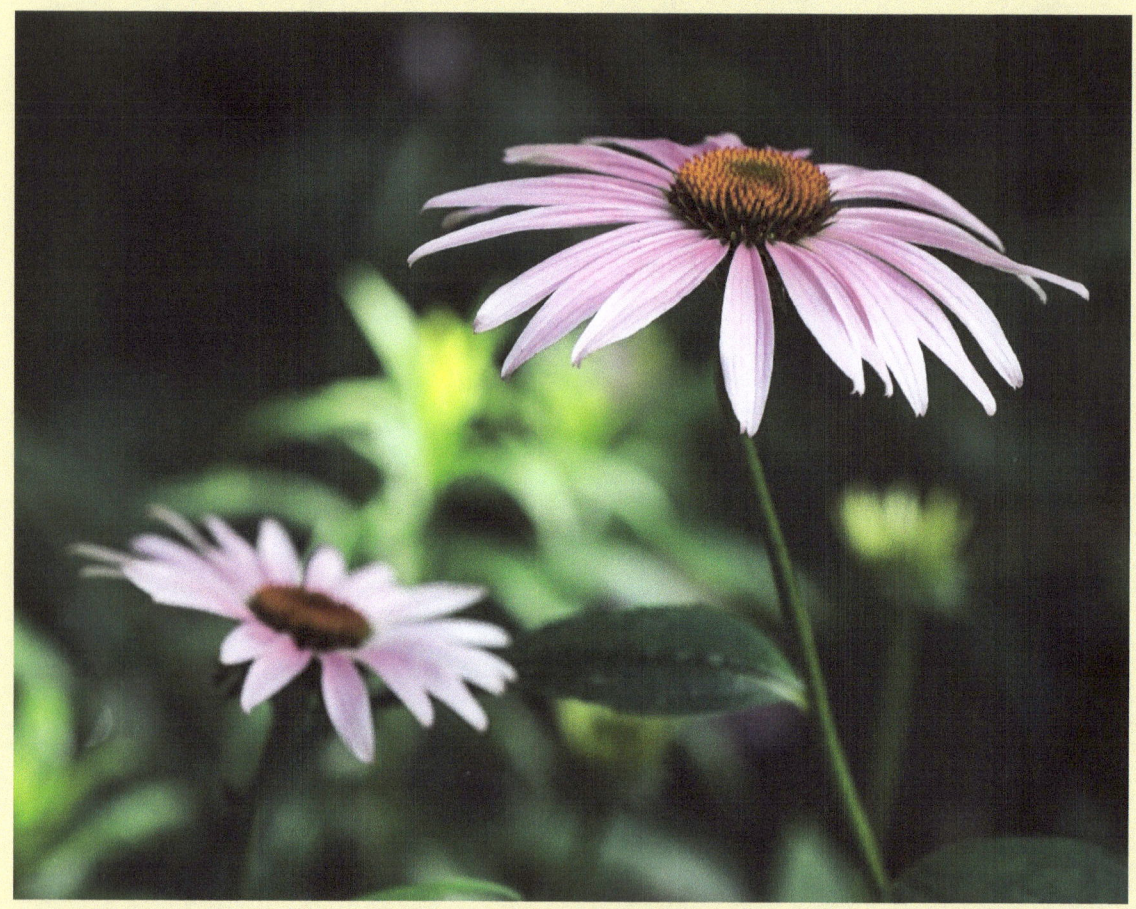

Photographer: Matt Kantecki
3 acres dedicated to TLC in 2008

This three acre parcel of ancient oak woodland lies in the heart of one of the largest remaining oak woodlands in McHenry County. Wildflowers of all shapes and sizes thrive in the understory.

Tauck Conservation Easement, Marengo Township

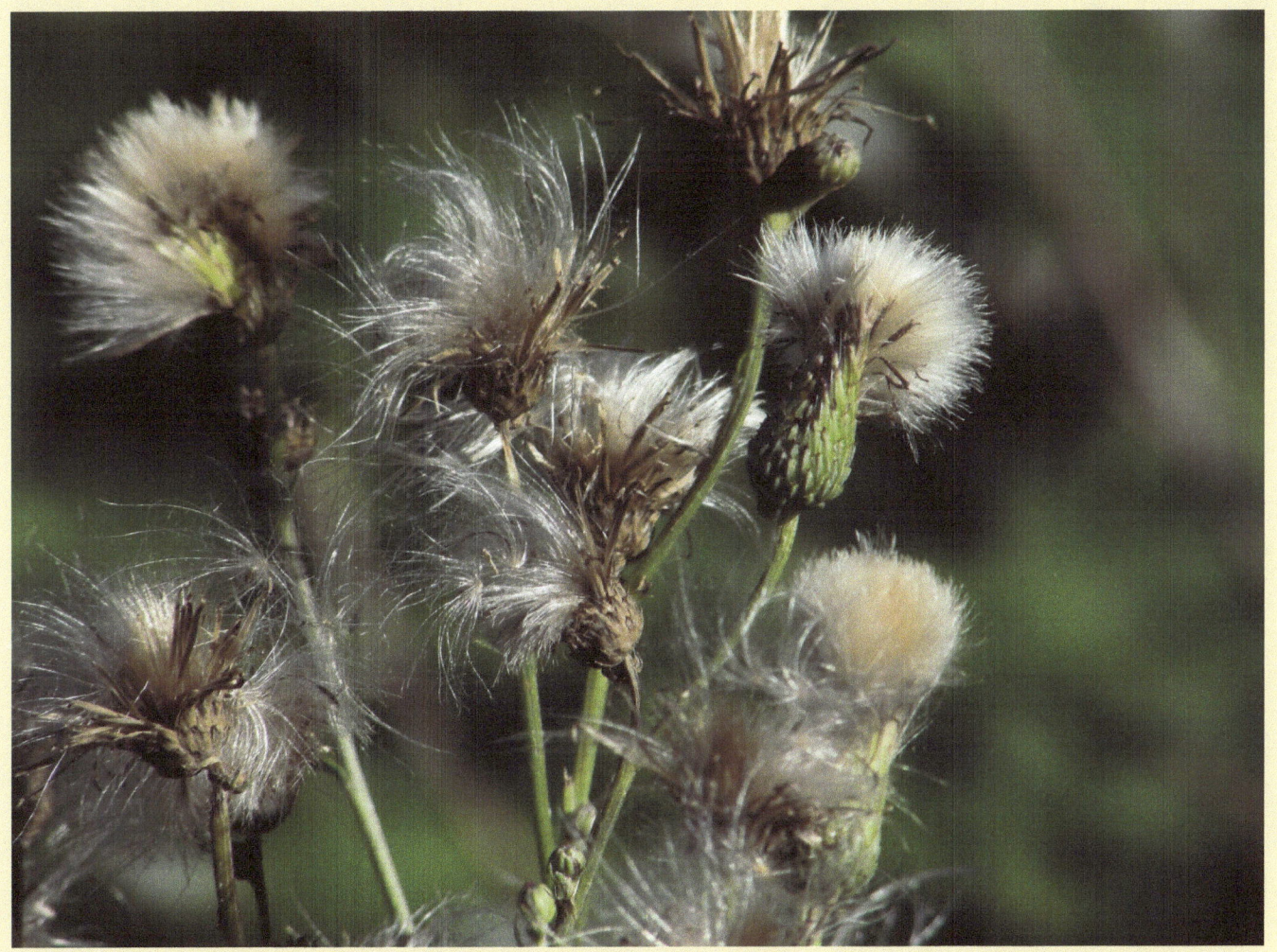

Photographer: Michael Fleck
61 acres dedicated to TLC in 2004

In the forty years Susan Tauck has lived on the property, she has been watching the native flora and fauna. The woodland and vernal pools of the easement have the most unusual plants, and the old horse and sheep pastures are slowly turning into an interesting prairie.

Trout Valley Fen, Trout Valley

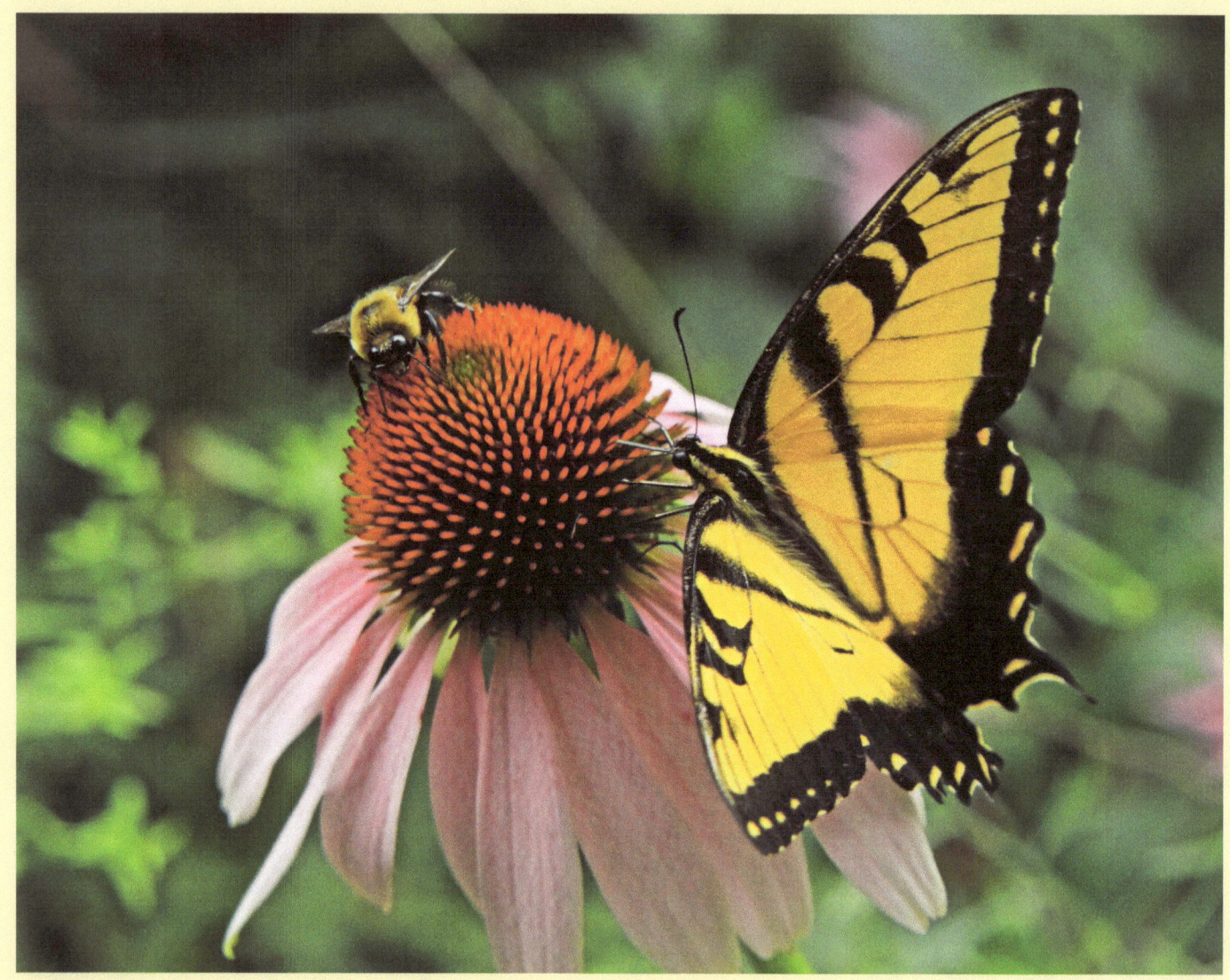

Photographer: Tiffany Whisler

9 acres owned by the Trout Valley Association, managed by TLC since 2015

Thankfully, this little known area was saved as a place for nature to be left alone. Walking paths allow people to access and enjoy this remnant fen and woodland .

Trout Valley Fen, Trout Valley

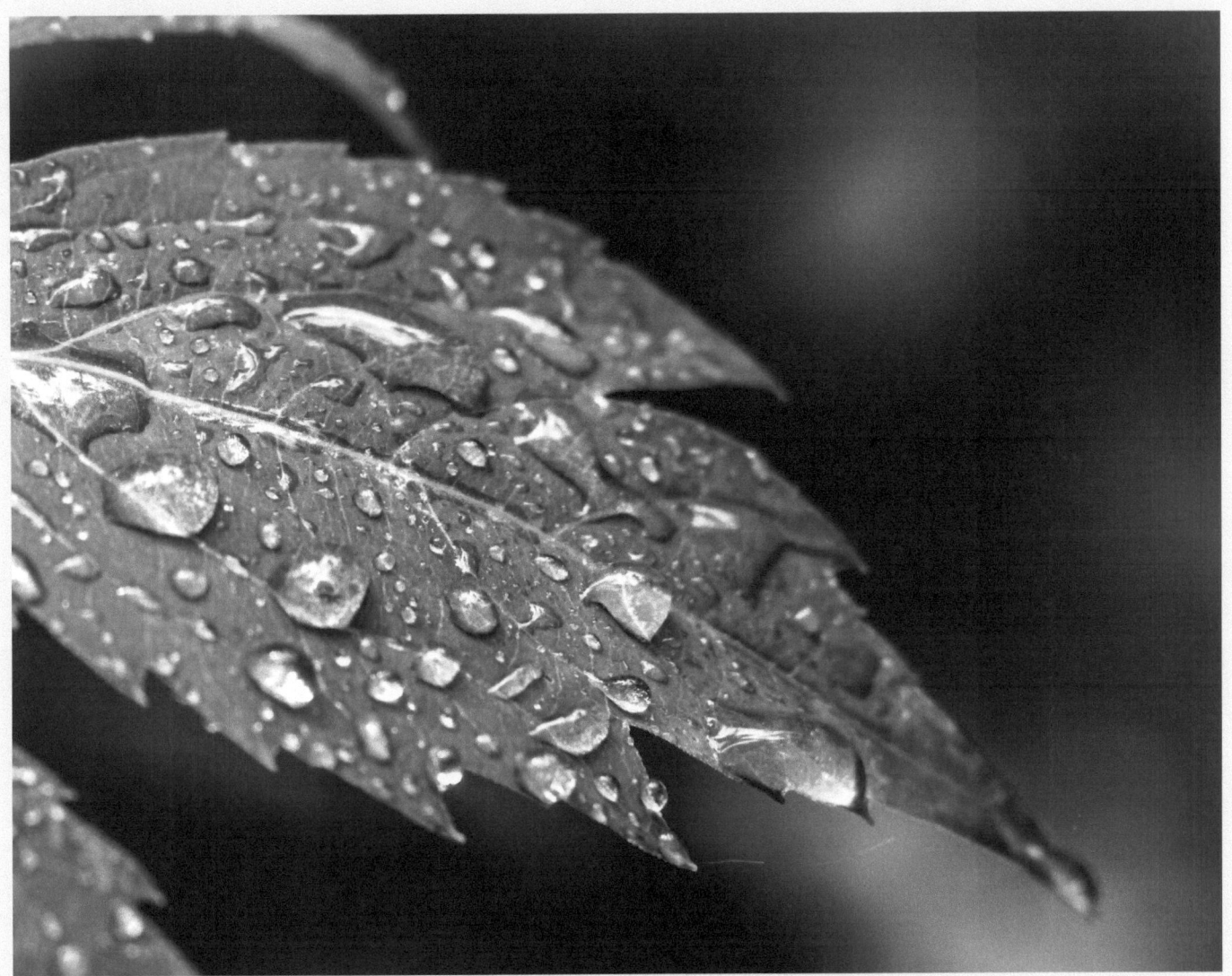

Photographer: Bob Williams
9 acres owned by the Trout Valley Association, managed by TLC since 2015

TLC recently partnered with the Village of Trout Valley to help restore and maintain this rare habitat. The rolling hills, springs, and shade create a unique habitat. In the bottoms you can find large patches of skunk cabbage- the first flower to bloom in early spring!

Van Maren Conservation Easement, Dunham Township

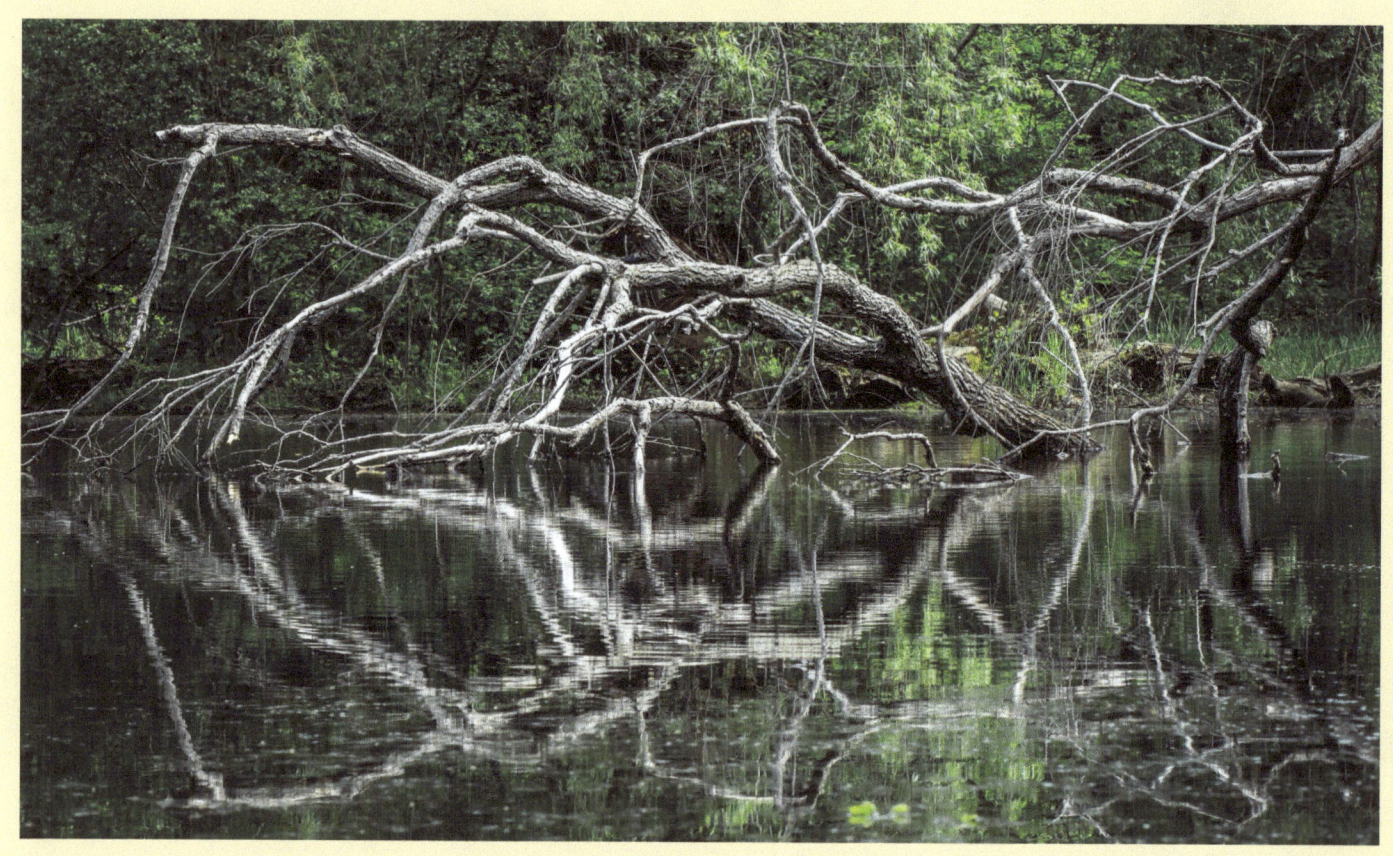

Photographer: Alan Smith
40 acres dedicated to TLC in 2013

When Al Van Maren donated an easement on his 40 acres of woods, it helped preserve one of the last large remnant oak woodlands in the county. This woodland is part of a joint effort between McHenry County Conservation District and TLC to preserve a total of 93 contiguous acres of old growth oaks.

Westwood Conservation Area, Woodstock

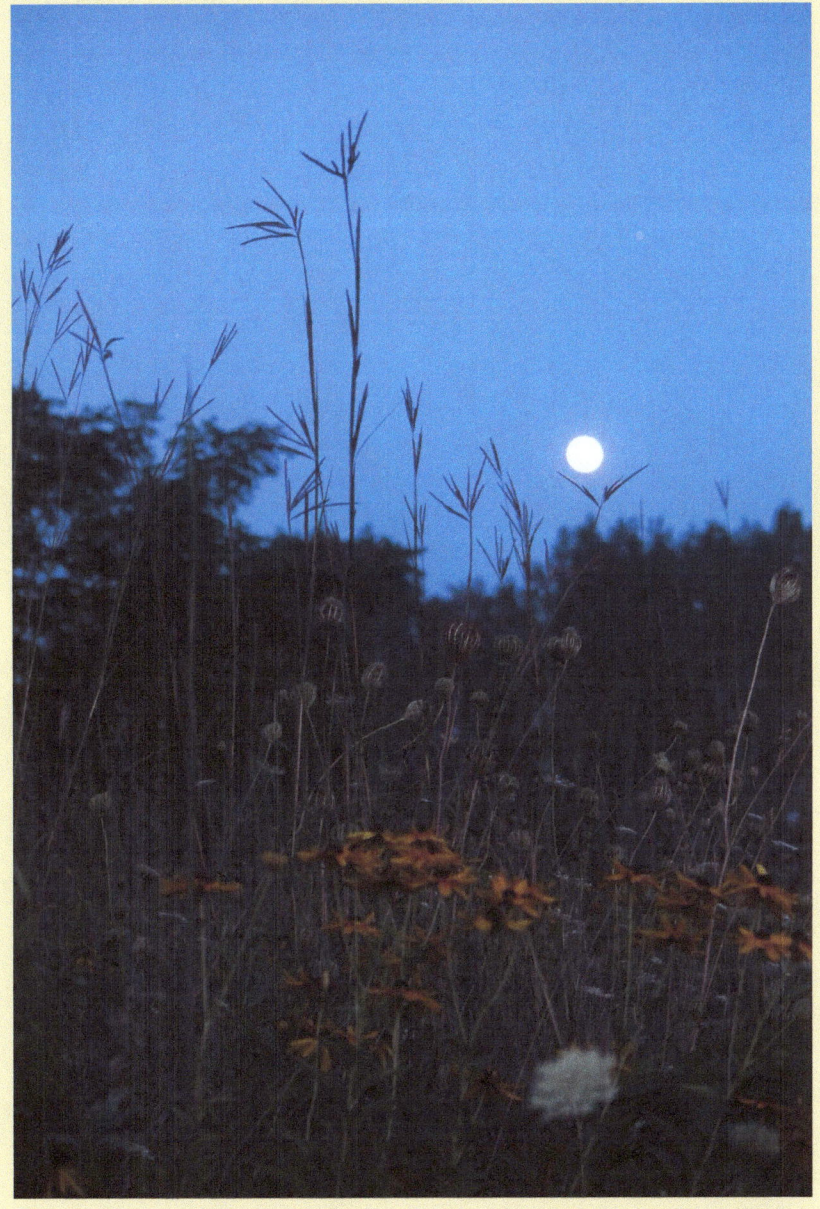

Photographer: Carolyn Sweeney
63 acres owned by the City of Woodstock, managed by TLC since 2006

In 2010 this property was dedicated as an Illinois Nature Preserve and buffer for the adjacent TLC Yonder Prairie. Restoration work has been underway for several years opening up the woodland full of massive oaks, and working along the edge to let it gently transition into prairie.

Wilson Conservation Easement, Lake in the Hills

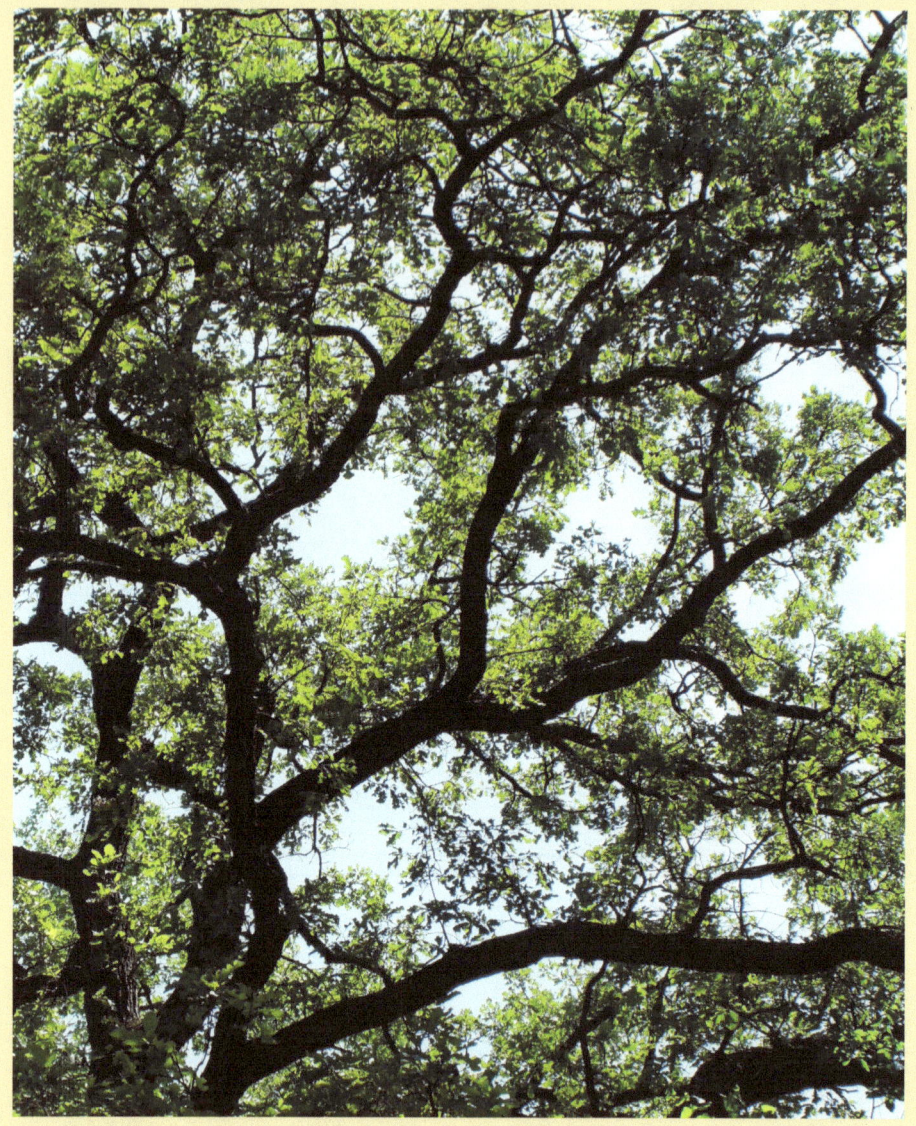

Photographer: Frank Freimuth
2 acres dedicated to TLC in 1999

You might not think "nature" in this area of the county, where strip malls, subdivisions, and roads abound. But in this back yard you'll find oaks, wildflowers, deer, and birds, just as they were centuries ago!

Windy Knoll Conservation Area, Nunda Township

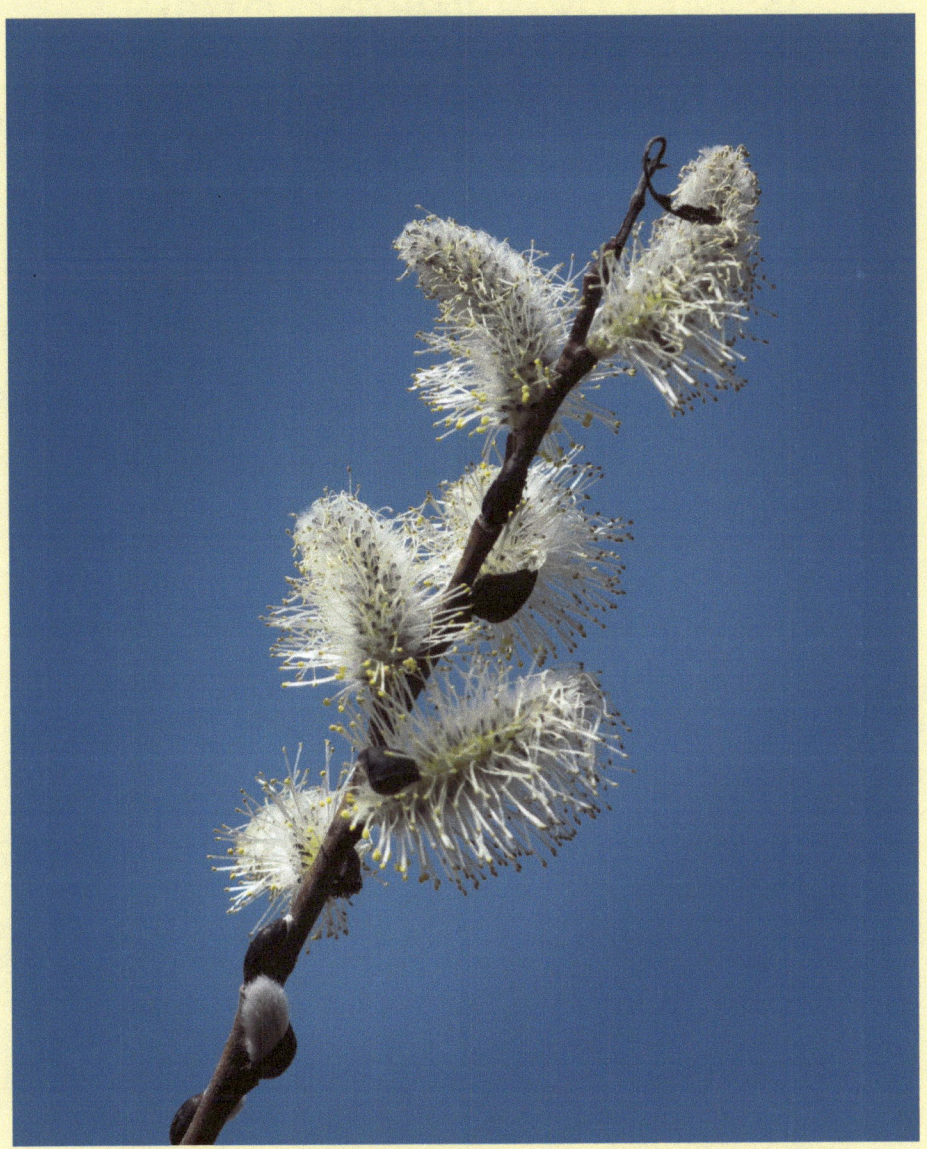

Photographer: Lisa Meinhard Sly
22 acres donated to TLC in 2002

Windy Knoll/Powers Creek was the first land donation that TLC accepted. This is another easement right in the middle of a subdivision, allowing residents easy access to nature just outside their front doors.

Wingate Conservation Easement, Nunda Township
Youth Photographer Award

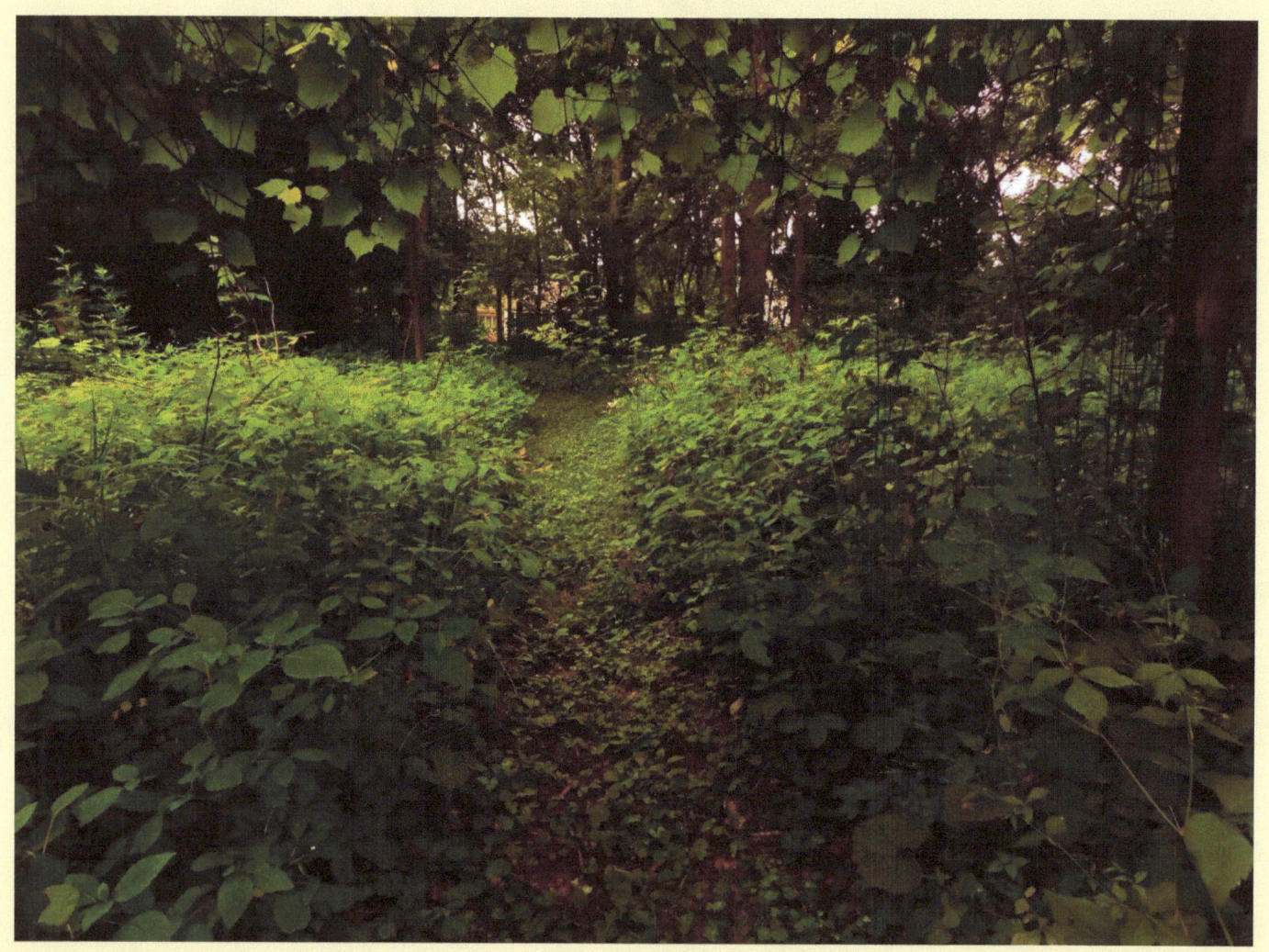

Photographer: Quinn Hankins
4 acres dedicated to TLC in 1994

Walking paths wind through oak trees and offer an astounding view of various wildflowers. Few backyards can boast the number of songbirds and other critters that also call this place home. Thanks to years of careful tending and the foresight to dedicate an easement, this backyard will remain natural in perpetuity.

Wingate Conservation Easement, Nunda Township

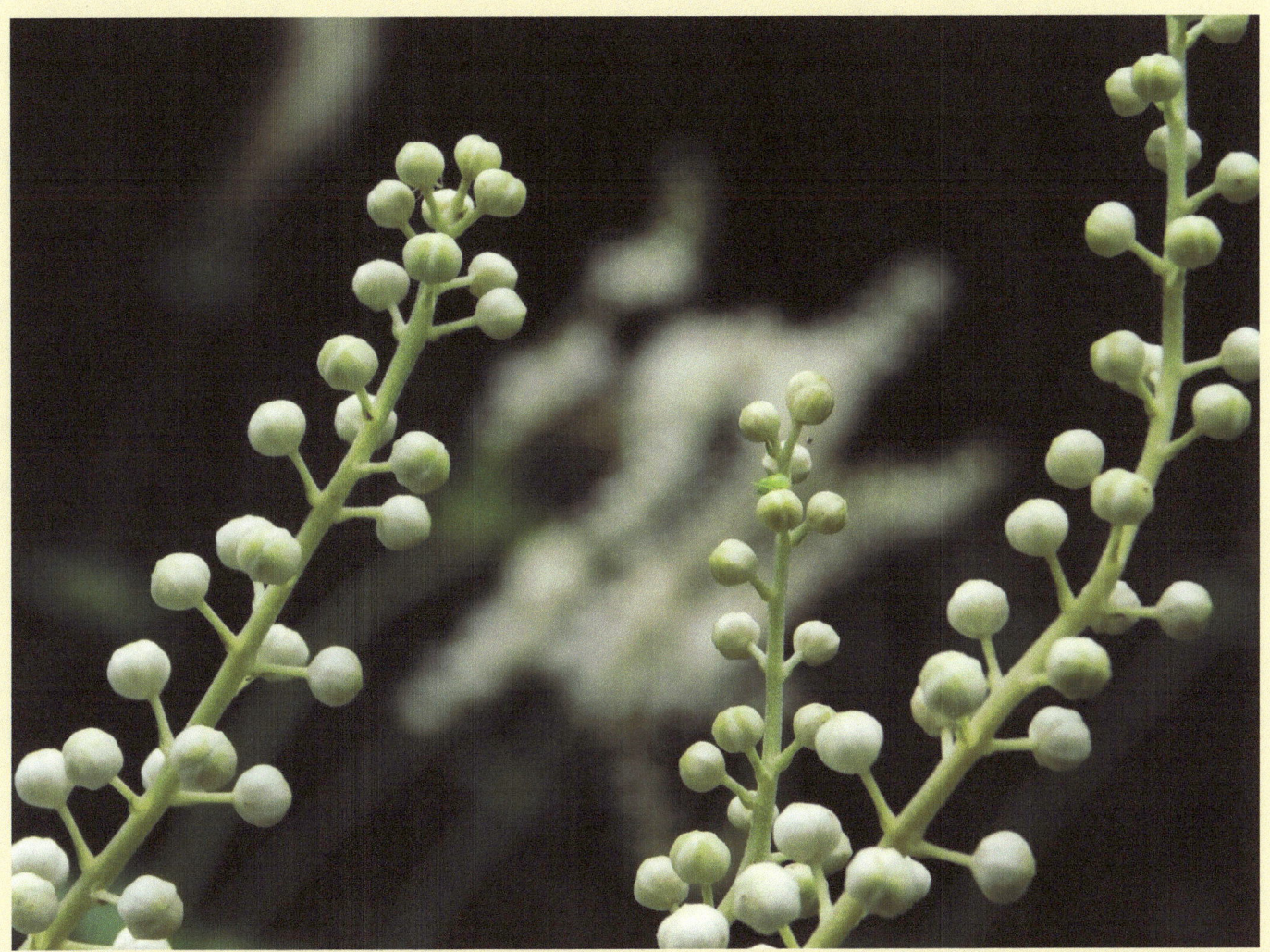

Photographer: Kim Hankins
4 acres dedicated to TLC in 1994

Landowners Randy and Nancy Schietzelt have done a phenomenal job continuing to care for the land that Bill Wingate tended. Nancy is currently the president of the Environmental Defenders of McHenry County, and Randy serves on the board for The Land Conservancy. You can usually find them putting in countless hours of work at an environmental event or restoration workday throughout the county.

Wingate Conservation Easement, Nunda Township

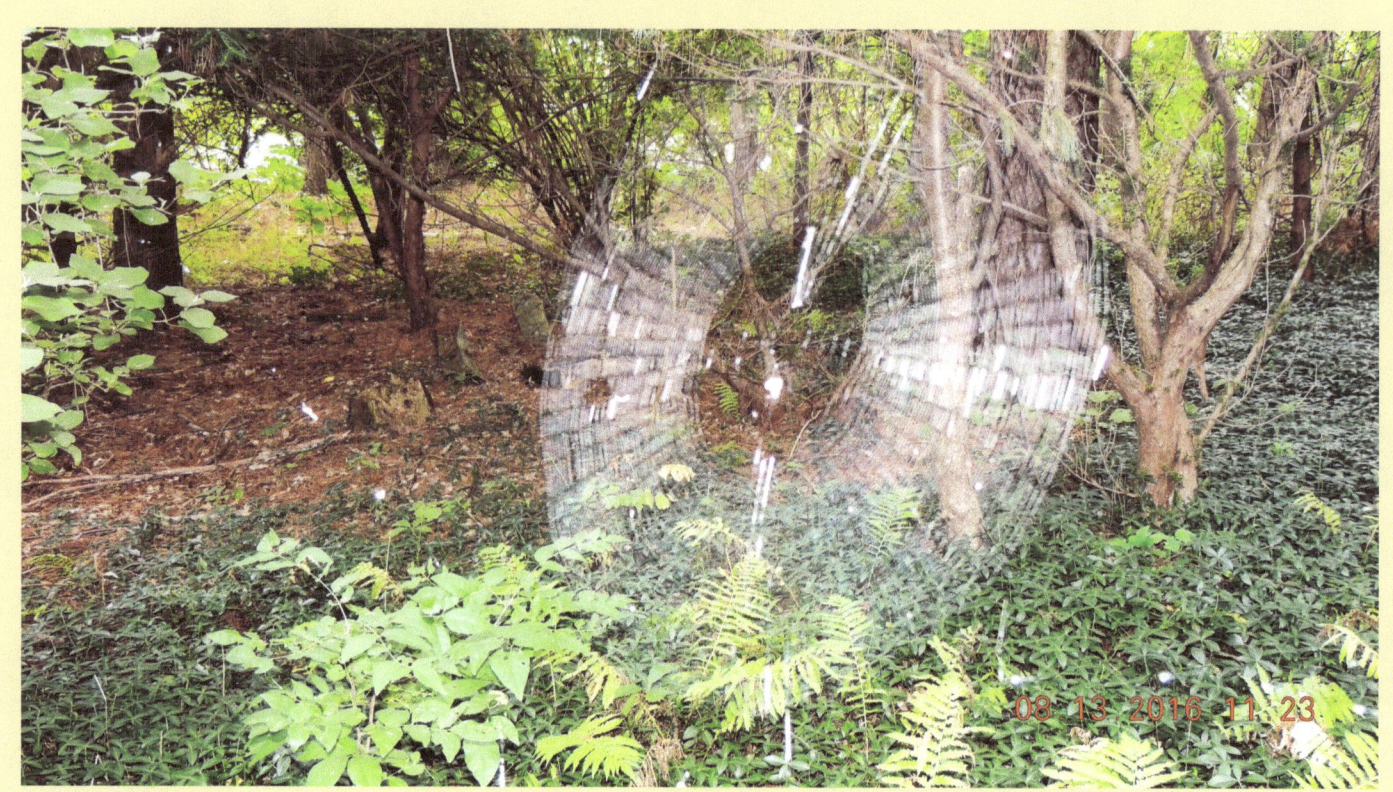

Photographer: Kathy Hammond
4 acres dedicated to TLC in 1994

Bill Wingate, famous for his "Wanders with Wingate" nature walks around McHenry County, lived on this property with his wife Ardath. They transformed their backyard into a wonderful place to enjoy their own nature walks, under the trees and along a stream.

Woodstock Center (Brookdale), Hartland Township

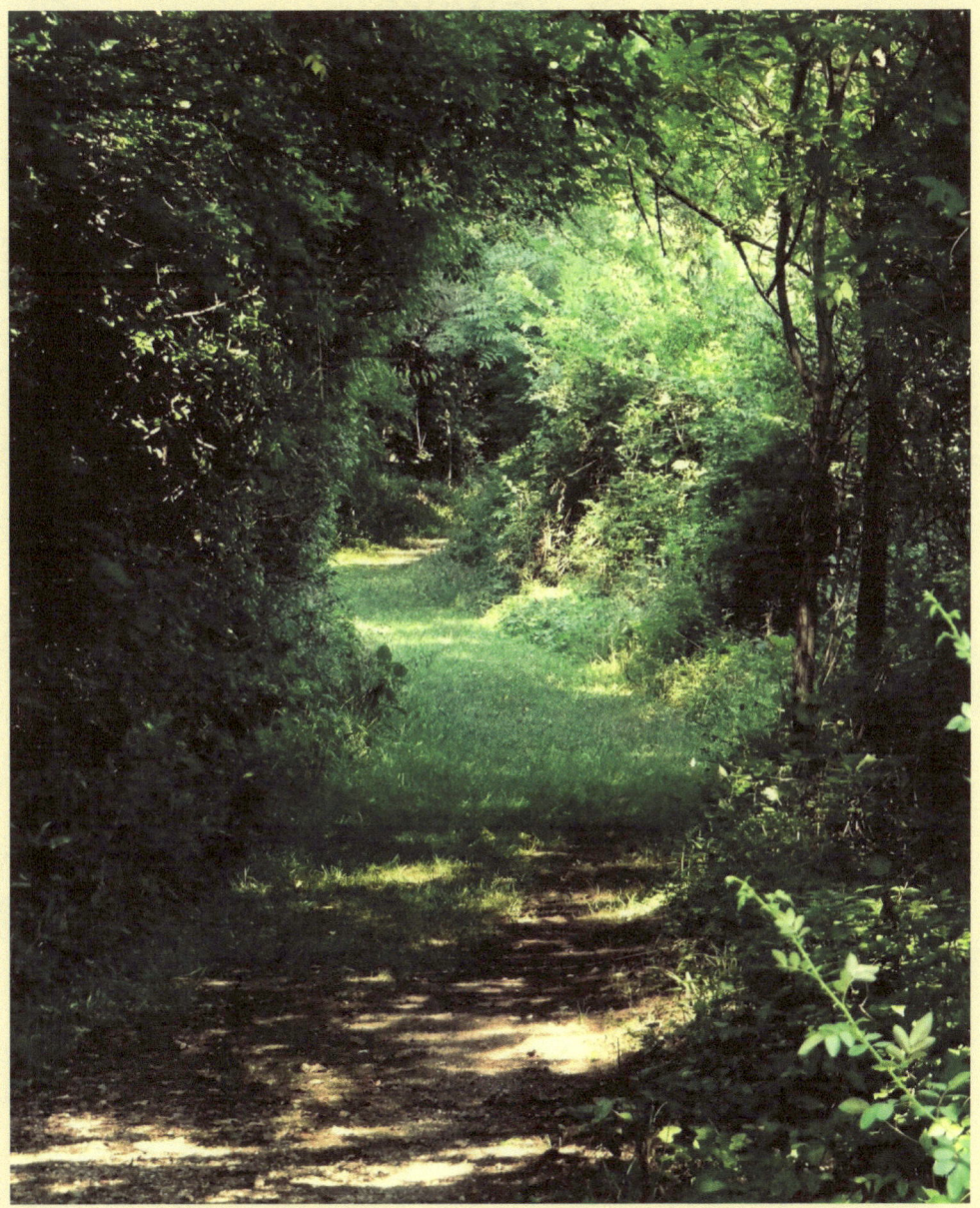

Photographer: Amy Peterson
65 acres dedicated to TLC in 1999

The Woodstock Center easement was donated by the Scheinfeld family at the same time the property was sold to McHenry County Conservation District. The property forms the nucleus for what has now become a 1200+ acre conservation area.

Yonder Prairie Nature Preserve Addition, Seneca Township

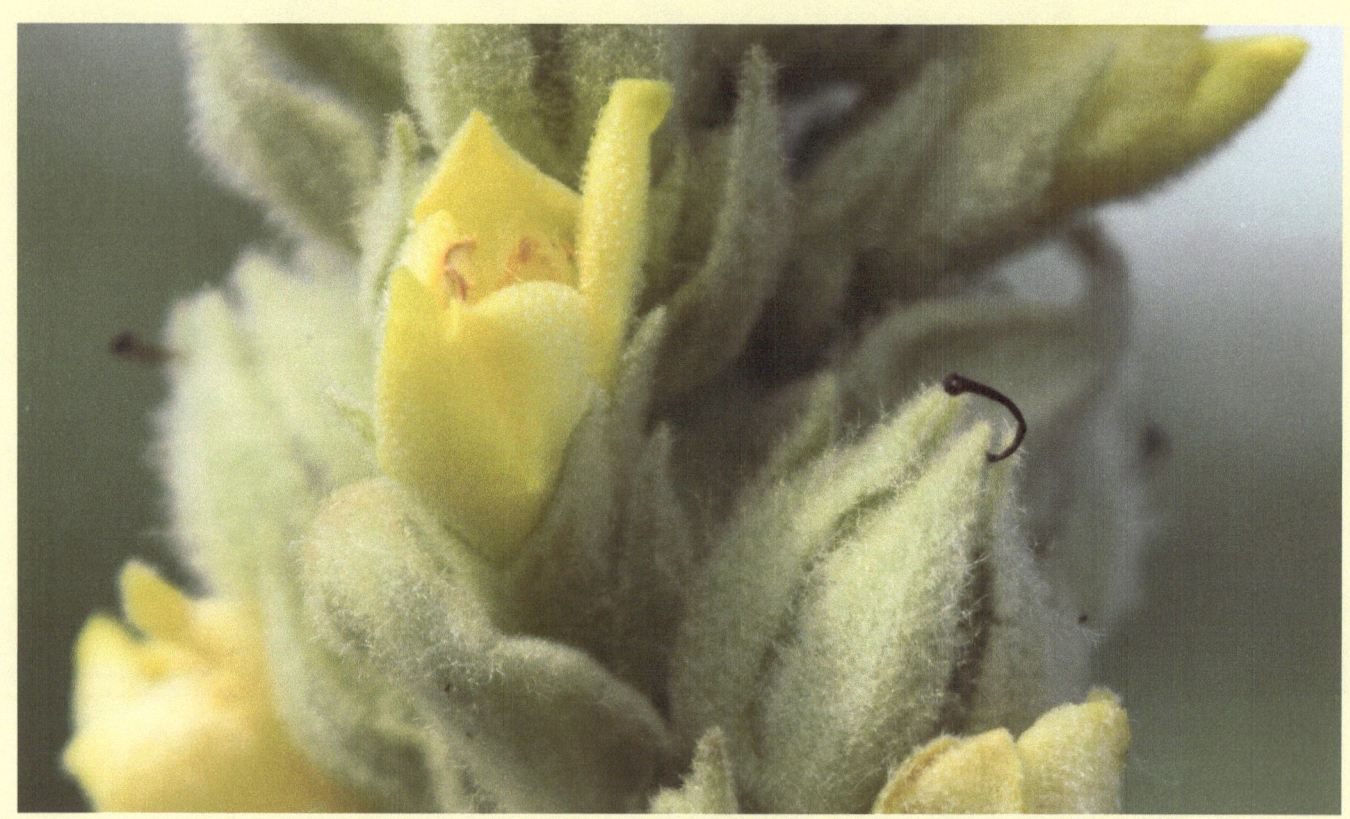

Photographer: Brianna Walneck
26 acres purchased by TLC in 2013

TLC has been adding onto the acreage of Yonder Prairie over the years, but this 26 acre addition is by far the largest. It features an oak grove, a restored prairie, and two high quality remnant wetlands.

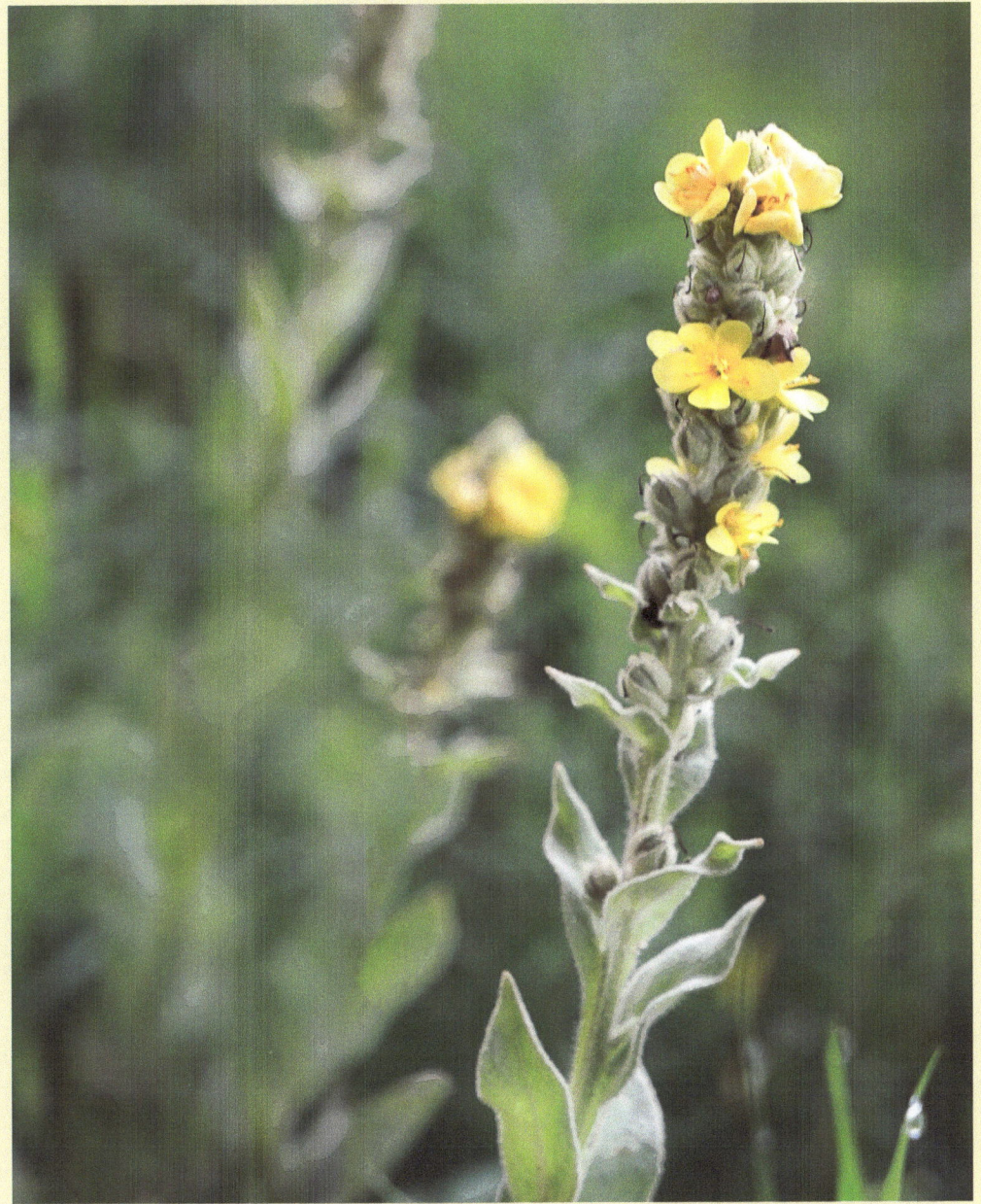

Photographer: Gail Moreland
40 acres purchased by TLC in 2008

Prior to the purchase of this land, it was deemed the highest quality unprotected natural area in the county. Now the complex of oak woodland, wet prairie and sedge meadow is classified as an Illinois Nature Preserve- the highest level of protection available to natural lands in the state.

Zoost-Weier Preserve, Nunda Township

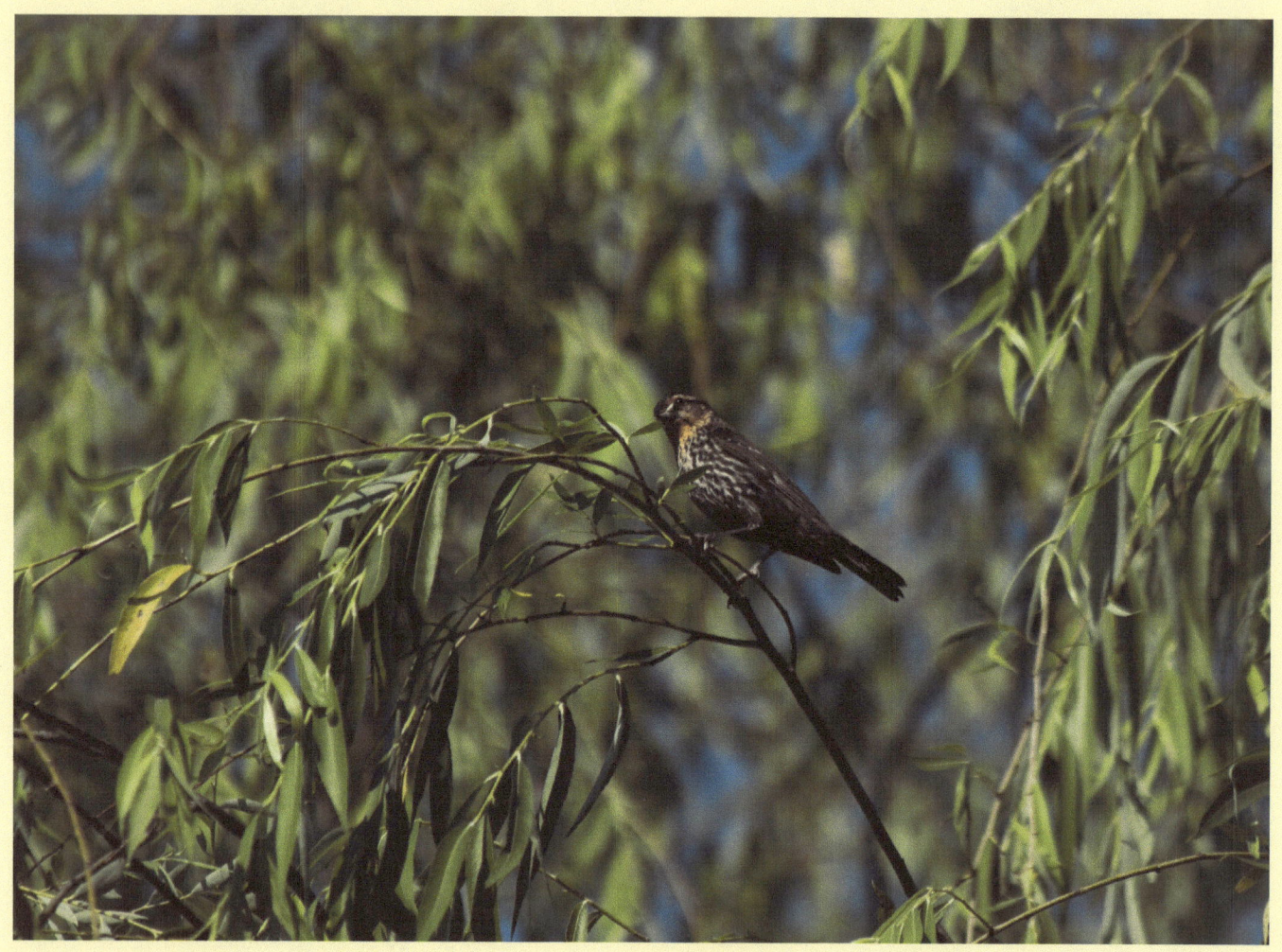

Photographer: Andrea Yori
4 acres donated to TLC in 2011

Although we didn't quite know what we would find on this small corner of land, we were surprised with the vast amount of high quality remnant plants that still called this place home. With the help of our volunteers, TLC has gotten right to work restoring it.

Information about TLC's 2016 Art of the Land Art Sale and Benefit

2016 was the eighth year for TLC's Art of the Land Art Sale and Benefit at the Starline Factory in Harvard. This two-night event, held in September, is a collaboration between artists from the region who find inspiration in the land and McHenry County's oldest non-profit land conservation organization: The Land Conservancy of McHenry County.

Art of the Land could not happen without the many talented artists who participate, and without the hundreds of guests who attend the event and purchase artwork. Thirty percent of all sales go to support TLC's land preservation mission.

A big thank you goes to Orrin and Karen Kinney, owners of the Starline Factory, who donate use of the space to TLC for the benefit, and donate the labor of several workers to help set up the space for this unique show.

Finally we are eternally grateful to the many volunteers who donate hundreds of hours (valued at several thousand dollars) during the months leading up to the event. Volunteers do everything from hanging artwork, installing lighting, painting walls, serving food, selling tickets, running raffles and sweeping floors. Quite simply, Art of the Land could not happen without the efforts of all the volunteers.

Please contact TLC about participating at a future event: 815-337-9502 or www.ConserveMC.org.

www.ingramcontent.com/pod-product-compliance
Lightning Source LLC
Chambersburg PA
CBHW050902180526
45159CB00007B/2761